Washington's Gardens at Mount Vernon

Washington's Gardens at Mount Vernon

LANDSCAPE OF THE INNER MAN

Mac Griswold

PHOTOGRAPHY BY ROGER FOLEY

A FRANCES TENENBAUM BOOK

HOUGHTON MIFFLIN COMPANY

BOSTON   NEW YORK   1999

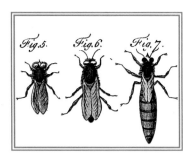

Half title: *May Duke Cherry* from
The Hot-House Gardener, by John
Abercrombie, London, 1789.

Frontispiece: The upper garden at
Mount Vernon.

Title page: Fruit trees in the upper garden.

Above: Bees from *The Complete Farmer,*
by a Society of Gentlemen, London,
1769 edition.

All works illustrated unless otherwise noted
are from the collections of the Mount
Vernon Ladies' Association of the Union.

For information about permission to reproduce selections from this book,
write to Permissions, Houghton Mifflin Company,
215 Park Avenue South, New York, NY 10003.

Library of Congress Cataloging-in-Publication Data

Griswold, Mac K.
Washington's Gardens at Mount Vernon: Landscape of the Inner Man / Mac
Griswold.
p. cm.
"A Frances Tenenbaum book."
Includes bibliographical references and index.
ISBN 0-395-92970-9
1. Mount Vernon Gardens (Va.) 2. Mount Vernon (Va. : Estate) 3. Washington, George, 1732–1799—
Contributions in gardening. 4. Washington, George, 1732–1799—Homes and haunts—Virginia—Fair-
fax Country. 5. Gardening—Virginia—Fairfax County—History—18th century. 6. Mount Vernon
Gardens (Va.)—Pictorial works. 7. Mount Vernon (Va. : Estate)—Pictorial works. 8. Washington,
George, 1732–1799—Homes and haunts—Virginia—Fairfax County—Pictorial works. I. Title.
E312.5.G83 1999
973.4'1'092—dc21   98-46015
CIP

Designed by Susan McClellan
Printed in Hong Kong
DNP 10 9 8 7 6 5 4 3 2 1

Acknowledgments

M Y INITIAL IMPULSE toward writing this book was entirely trivial and selfish. When I first heard of the project, I understood at once that it implied overnights at Mount Vernon alone, "doing research" after the gates had closed, when only the wild turkeys, mules, and security trucks were circulating about the place, along with fog rising from the river. It was Dean Norton, today's gardener at Mount Vernon (he is the thirty-fourth in the line) who first raised the idea, three years ago, and to him go my thanks for the opportunity, along with thanks for help all along the way. At Mount Vernon I would also like to thank King Laughlin, the curator, who provided the most outré but appropriate props for every photoshoot, and Christine Meadows, the former curator, who walked me around Mount Vernon on my first visit, quoting Washington extempore, and laying the groundwork for my understanding.

At the start of the project Barbara McMillan, the Mount Vernon librarian, thought of useful sources before I even imagined their existence and, in the last rushed month before I submitted the manuscript, found in her manicured collections the endnote citations that I had lost in a laptop disaster. She and Dennis Pogue, John Riley, and Mary Thompson all read the manuscript and made helpful and pointed suggestions and corrections. Sandra Robinette smoothed every access. In the gardens, Theresa Keiser told me how they do things now, contributing enormously to the "how-to" sections. At Mount Vernon James Rees, the resident director, Margaret Alison, the vice-regent for the state of Washington, and Carew Rice Lee, the regent and my friend from years ago, all performed vital operations, without which the book would never have taken shape.

My dear friends Susan Rowland and Stephen Kossak read parts of the manuscript and put up with my defensive evil temper when I first heard their entirely helpful and clever ideas for improvement. Victoria Hughes patiently listened, evening after evening at dinners in Sag Harbor, and asked me questions that let me hope that maybe it wouldn't be a totally boring read after all. Paula Deitz, Mark Laird, Lois Underhill, and others cheered me with valuable tidbits along the way. Mary Laing cast her experienced eye over the text.

ECHINACEA PURPUREA

*From **Curtis' Botanical Magazine**, Vol. 1, London, 1793.*

MOUNT VERNON FARE

At Houghton Mifflin, Frances Tenenbaum, my editor, loved the book from the proposal stage and adroitly steered it through all the rites of passage.

Lisa White, Houghton's peerless copyeditor, gently straightened out the crooked bits. Susan McClellan, the book's designer, gave it a shape that surely must suit even George himself, in heroes' heaven.

Roger Foley, the photographer whose book this is as much as it is mine, was the most intuitive of interpreters, grasping the need to get past iconic images to find a more kinetic vision. He hung himself from cherry pickers, waited for hours for sheep to turn their unsightly butts away from the camera, and always caught the moment when the light paled or flooded just the right objects and spaces.

I'd like to thank Jeffrey Posternak, my agent at Andrew Wylie, Inc., for whom illustrated garden books were an entirely new field, but who nonetheless handled it all with an effective mix of cautiousness and swashbuckling "why not?"–type action.

This is a book that also came out of my own memories. For a love of country life of a certain intricate and pleasantly ramshackle kind, I thought of my own parents, and of our New Jersey acres where my father, a Depression-era Texan and a Cold War-period chemical engineer during the week, dug fence-line postholes on the weekends and smoked our own hams in the whitewashed smokehouse. I shelled peas and lima beans and pitted cherries in the courtyard with my mother, my sister, and with Ella Fleming, who would freeze or can anything that moved. Boarding school gave me winters in Virginia, with frozen red mud and the occasional relief of mild days. My former parents-in-law, Ben and Leith Griswold, and the way they live in Monkton, Maryland, also made vivid many things I found in Washington's diaries and correspondence.

Most of all I thank Frederick Seidel, who encouraged me in the thought that this really was a broader, more biographical subject than I understood it to be, and told me to get serious and to write like a grownup, relying more than I had before on the power of suggestion and understatement. His greatest gifts were the willingness to read revisions more often than anyone should have to and a subtitle that concentrates the drift of all seven chapters into a single phrase.

Contents

A WHEELBARROW

From The Compleat Florist: The Universal Culture of Flowers, Trees and Shrubs Proper to Embellish Gardens . . . , by Louis Liger d'Auxerre, London, 1706.

WASHINGTON'S GARDENS AT MOUNT VERNON

CHAPTER ONE

A Plantation Portrait

"No Virginian can talk on any Subject, but the perfections of

Genl. Washington. It Weaves itself into every conversation. . . .

At his farm . . . the hands, Horses, Cattle to be used in tillage

& pasturage are arranged in a Roster calculated for 10 Years . . .

not a day's work, but is noted What, by Whom, and Where done,

not a Cow calves or Ewe drops her lamb, but is registered. Thus

the etiquette and arrangement of an army is preserved on his farm.

But is it not nature? When once the human mind is penetrated

by any System, no matter What, It can never disengage itself . . ."

THE DIARY OF WILLIAM MACLAY, MAY 1, 1790
Washington was serving his first presidential term.

GEORGE WASHINGTON,
BY CHARLES WILSON PEALE, 1776

Sensitive and serious is how Washington appears in this miniature painted when he was forty-four — perhaps especially serious because in 1775 he had left his Virginia country life of building, gardening, and farming to take command of the ragged revolutionary army.

Opposite: THE WEST, OR ENTRANCE FRONT, FRAMED IN SPRING GREEN TREES

"A country house of an elegant and majestic simplicity" is how J. P. Brissot de Warville, a French visitor, described Mount Vernon in 1788. The same words were often used to describe George Washington himself.

IT IS ALL TOO EASY TO THINK ABOUT GEORGE WASHINGTON quite respectfully but without genuine interest, as if he actually were only Mount Rushmore: as unknowable and unmoving as a face carved out of a cliff. Always, the biographical question is "Who is he, really?" Today, "really" means "privately." A post-psychoanalytic age presents the spontaneous remark, the slip, the bleep, as the real truth about a

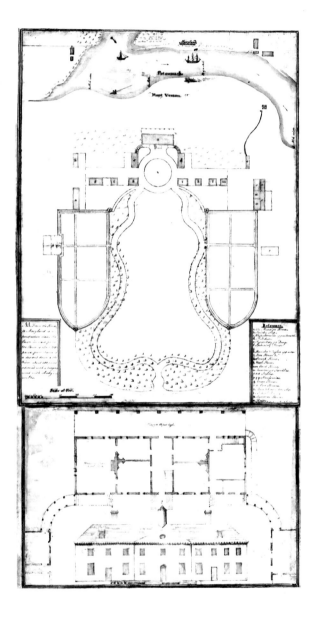

person — what goes on behind the façade. Anyone who thinks everything through before saying it, who makes plans carefully and then carries them out, seems curiously unreal. More believeable are rough edges, open doubts, conflicts displayed and resolved. That's very unlike Washington's carefully shaped decorum and measured self-awareness. He is, after all, the man who copied out maxims from a book of manners at the age of sixteen. What can he possibly have to say to us today? What was he really thinking?

By 1992 Washington had dropped to third in a "presidential greatness poll" taken among 900 historians: Lincoln and FDR had both outstripped him, perhaps just because he is so hard to know. The historian Gordon S. Wood writes, "He seems to come from another time and another place — from another world. And that's the whole point about him: he does come from another world. . . . He is the only truly classical hero we have ever had. . . . And he knew it. . . . That awareness of his heroic stature . . . affected nearly everything he did for the rest of his life." We resent that. Oh why can't he forget who he is for just a minute and let us in on the secret George Washington?

IF THERE IS ONE PLACE we can find the secret George, it's in his designing, gardening, and farming at Mount Vernon. He's undoubtedly the same George, but he seems more approachable here, doing what many of us do today, gardening and thinking a lot about it. Mount Vernon is Washington's self-portrait of himself as an American: dignified yet fashionable, productive, temperate, observant, even scientific — though not scholarly — and above all domestic. In this passionate domesticity we can all identify with the man.

If we are gardeners, we love Washington for his determined forty-five years of dedication to Mount Vernon (1754-99). The arts of gardening he practiced with his own hands are what we do too: designing, propagating, pruning, seed-gathering, planting and transplanting, even grafting. They telescope the distance between him and us.

We may especially feel close to him when he failed. In 1785 he carefully sowed a precious gift, the seeds of two hundred Chinese species, in his own little botanical garden where he did most of the work himself. The next year, he reported "None... were to be seen," a success rate of zero. Even a hero must put up with misfortune. Though many gardens are now "installed" in a week — the sod unrolled, the thirty-foot-trees craned in — it's not sentimental to say that the best gardens still only become "best" with time and personal involvement.

The RESTORED GARDENS of Mount Vernon are handsome and peaceful. They are laid out in five separate areas: besides the botanical garden, they are the upper garden, which evolved into a pleasure garden; the lower, or kitchen garden; the vineyard enclosure, mostly fruit trees and experimental plantings of different grass crops, grains, and vegetables; and the landscape garden, the setting of lawns and views and groves, the eighteenth century's signature design.

At first glance, this all seems as moderate and balanced as does Washington himself. Yet these carefully created (and now re-created) surroundings erupt occasionally in such an abundance of kinds of trees, or patterns of flowers, or volleys of views both short and long, that we feel the spontaneous delight the man took such pains to discipline and control. These gardens embody Washington's urge to make something perfect and beautiful against all odds, and there are no odds greater than the intractable realities of soil, setting, and the seasons themselves, as every gardener knows.

Mount Vernon's landscape also wordlessly portrays Washington's hopes for his new nation. We are aware of orchards; fields of grain; enclosures overflowing with fruits, vegetables, and flowers; tall trees; the green bluff over the shining river; the long straight view from the house back toward the front gates — Washington's carefully laid-out "visto" — westward to America's future. It is all as idyllic and prosperous as Washington so ardently wanted his new country to be.

The evolution of Mount Vernon as a working farm also chronicles Washington's concept of independence, a tale of changing economic policy and political thought, both for him personally as a farmer and landowner, and as the best-known and most revered national public figure for a quarter of a century, from the time he became commander in chief until his death in 1799.

Opposite: THE VAUGHAN PLAN, PRESENTED TO GEORGE WASHINGTON BY HIS FRIEND AND ADMIRER, SAMUEL VAUGHAN, IN 1787

The house and its dependencies, or outbuildings, look small compared to the domestic landscape surrounding them. More prominent are the outlines of the gardens, shaped like pointed arches, or ogives, and the central bowling green, bounded by the swooping curves of serpentine walks. The ground-floor plan and the entrance elevation of "Home House," as Washington called it, are seen below on the plan.

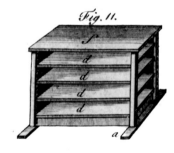

A BEE FRAME

*From **The Complete Farmer** (London, 1769 edition), by a Society of Gentlemen, an English agricultural dictionary owned by Washington.*

For a long time now it has been impossible to think about American history without considering the fact of slavery, even when the subject is George Washington — perhaps especially when it is George Washington. He did not make his gardens alone. About 200 able-bodied men and women (the total slave force was 316 in 1799) actually created and tended Mount Vernon. His Home Farm's work force of about ninety, the "Mansion House people," lived near the main house. Some of their labors seem heartbreakingly inhumane. For instance, trees were transplanted in winter when the ground was frozen. This ensured a better survival rate for the trees because winter is when they are dormant, but it was much harder on those who chopped the rock-hard soil. Contextual explanations about labor practices or economic dependence on slavery cannot lighten its shadow, especially at a time and among leaders so concerned with individual liberty. But we can note Washington's own intellectual and moral struggles with the institution, which finally amounted to more than talk. "...to disperse the families I have an aversion," he said, refusing to separate families by selling them. He would free all his own slaves at his death, the only one of the slaveholding founding fathers to do so.

How do we know any of this? Luckily for us, Washington spent many years away from home. During the two terms of his presidency, for instance, he visited Mount Vernon only fifteen times. Determined to manage efficiently from afar, he left streams of letters and directives about every aspect of the place. He also kept a diary, and his hired gardeners left weekly accounts, some of which have survived. Visitors noted everything they recalled about their visits; Mount Vernon was soil sacred to memory.

So there are hundreds of things we can learn about this man in his gardens, this pioneer farmer, this modern Cincinnatus. We know he collected young trees he especially admired in the wild, such as dogwood and redbud, classic plants of Virginia's piedmont woodland. He loved the pink flowers and sculpted foliage of what he called "ivy," the mountain laurel. From a surprised visitor's account we know he threw off his coat to dig and plant himself. He stepped off and surveyed his own measurements for buildings and grounds. On his travels, he remembered the details he saw and reinterpreted them in his own house and gardens. He was almost always able to control his legendary temper, but he got cross when the seeds he directed to be planted

Opposite: Looking over the Potomac

The blue river view remains the same; dogwood **(Cornus florida)** *and redbud* **(Cercis canadensis)** *spangle the green slope beneath a chestnut oak that probably dates to Washington's day.*

Now you see it, now you don't

Movement along one of the serpentines around the bowling green reveals tantalizing flashes of color in spring, such as this redbud silhouetted against an old brick garden wall.

Washington often transplanted this tall evergreen June-flowering shrub, mountain laurel, which he called "ivy," into his gardens from the Virginia woodlands.

Opposite: A GARDEN DRUGSTORE

Herbs were used in the Washingtons' kitchen, but also distilled or made into ointments for medicinal purposes. Onions, a favorite vegetable, were also used to cure colds and kill worms. Standing ready are a tin measuring cup and the stone mortar and pestle that have always been at Mount Vernon. Common eighteenth-century herbs include lavender, basil, rosemary, and parsley flakes in the bowl at left, with bay leaves and black pepper, right. "Cayan pepper" in the small bowl at center, was ordered by Washington from the West Indies and later planted in his little botanical garden.

in his absence didn't get into the ground. He managed to make modest amounts of money as a farmer in Virginia when most men of his age and class were losing it, or moving west. Mount Vernon, even in its final state, is modest by comparison with the huge James River plantations and early Georgian houses, foursquare and brick, built in Washington's youth, such as Berkeley, Shirley, and Westover. The surprise of Mount Vernon face to face, as it was with the man, is that it is quite modest and graceful, but full of dignity.

VISITORS IN WASHINGTON'S DAY had the chance to measure this living portrait against the living model. After arriving at the plantation by river or land, they saw the packet boat continue on, or the horses led off to be watered, and their baggage carried upstairs, if they were spending the night. Then there might be a sighting of the tall, imposing, and famous personage himself, fresh from his farm rounds in a blue coat, white cashmere waistcoat, and slightly spattered black breeches and boots. Or of Martha Washington, the affable, dignified woman of whom one visitor said, ". . . she well deserved to be the companion and friend of the greatest man of the age."

Descriptions of her varied, often depending on the observer's expectations. "She is small and fat, her appearance is respectable," wrote a young Frenchman, Claude Blanchard, in 1782. Blanchard had perhaps imagined someone more aristocratic, more in keeping with the notion of a European prince's consort. "She was dressed very plainly," he continues, "and her manners were simple in all respects; she had with her three other ladies, her relations." Some court, perhaps he thought to himself. Seven years later, the acute and often unkind Abigail Adams, John Adams' wife, would present another view of Mrs. Washington as First Lady, when she met her in New York City: "She is plain in her dress, but that plainess is the best of every article. Her Hair is white, her Teeth beautiful, her person rather short than otherways. . . Her manners are modest and unassuming, dignified and femenine, not a tincture of ha'ture about her." In and around the house also were various members of the Custis and Washington families, private secretaries and other employees, and, always, the house slaves.

"I should enjoy more real happiness in one month with you at home than I have the most distant prospect of finding abroad, if my stay were to be seven times seven years," he wrote to her from Philadelphia on the eve of his departure for New England as commander in chief of the Continental Army.

Martha Washington, the domestic circle, and George, even the secret George, all fall within imaginative reach, thanks to such many-layered sources. What is harder to grasp — as hard as the institution of slavery and what it meant on a day-to-day basis — is how differently the landscape and gardens once fit into the plantation whole. Now, they seem like the ornamental climax of a polished design. Then they stood in paradisical contrast to the noise, filth, stench, and apparent chaos of a working plantation.

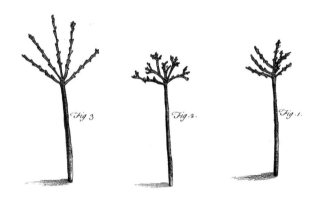

SEVERE PRUNING

During the years after the war when Washington was most occupied with planting his new landscape, he spent hours pruning his new, young trees. From **A Treatise of Fruit-Trees**, *by Thomas Hitt, London, 1757.*

The gardens were necessary: a cornucopia of plenty for the kitchen, a medicine chest, and a lab for economic botany. Beyond the purely practical, they served other purposes as well. The grounds, the fifty acres or so immediately surrounding the house, were also part of the garden, not in any productive meaning of the word, but in the eighteenth-century sense of "landscape garden." Its "well-gravel'd" paths,

EARLY MORNING MIST

A visitor to Mount Vernon's crowded rooms would have found solitude along these walks, where the fog turns the distant colonnade into a memory of tree trunks.

Washington's pride, were meant for hospitable walks, private conversation, and perhaps even solitude, a rare commodity in eighteenth-century life. The design of the whole and the presence in the conservatory of exotic plants from every part of the world usefully indicated the Washingtons' high level of taste, status, fashion, and power. And, in the sense that gardens since the beginnings of recorded time have

been emblems of safety and delight, Mount Vernon's gardens were an oasis in the American wilderness.

*T*F WE WANT TO GET BACK TO THE REALITY of that plantation, past the clean, sanitized "Country Club Mount Vernon," that necessarily exists today, we must walk through the grounds using the eyes, ears, and noses of the past. Outside the center hall door to the east is the tall, shady piazza, the connection between the house and its landscape that Washington himself designed. Ninety feet long, it is his most enduring and recognizable architectural legacy. The squared Tuscan piers (cheaper and easier for a plantation carpenter to make than round columns) frame the famously spectacular view of the Potomac River, whose silver surface, 137 feet below, sometimes thrashes with sturgeon swimming upstream, or is blackened with thousands of ducks. River boats, both passenger and commercial, tack back and forth. Merchants' vessels transport tobacco, the life support that made colonial Virginians rich and impoverished their soil.

To the north of the house, behind the elegant grove of locust trees picturesquely "planted without any order or regularity," comes the clang of a hammer on the anvil in the plantation blacksmith shop, the hiss of hot iron tempered in cold water, the sharp, rotten smell of horses' hooves pared for shoeing. Only a hundred feet south of the house — and never mentioned in any description of Mount Vernon, perhaps for propriety's sake, or because it was such an expected sight? — is a twenty-year-old trash heap, or midden, twenty-five feet across. Washington's foxhounds, some homebreds, some from England and France, gifts from admirers, can be heard mourning softly in their kennel closer to the river.

Around the south corner of the house, past the south grove "of all the clever trees (especially flowering ones) that can be got," are the stables that finish the line of plantation outbuildings to the south. Horses are snorting quietly in their stalls, munching hay, hooves creaking on their straw bedding. Mules, the offspring of Washington's prized Spanish jackass, "Royal Gift," bray in the turnout shed built into the lower slope of the barn. The compost heap sends up clouds of ammonia from its handsome roofed "stercorary," or dung pit, across the lane from the stable.

VIEW FROM THE PIAZZA

Two stories tall, the high pillars channel summer breezes and frame a distant boat on the Potomac. The trees clothing the steep slope whose tops hedge the east lawn were called a "hanging wood," a feature admired by eighteenth-century landscape gardeners.

Below: FLOWERING WILD BLACK LOCUST
TREES IN MAY

*In 1785 Washington had 133 horses on the five
farms, including his beloved old warhorses, Nelson
and Blueskin, retired to pasture from the fields
of battle.*

Right: THE NORTH GROVE

*Even before the branches of the black locusts
(**Robinia pseudoacacia**) leaf out, their thickly
planted trunks and evergreen American hollies
(**Ilex opaca**) do what Washington intended:
screen the north lane, a noisy, pungent work
area, from the house itself.*

Ted Vaughan

EYOND THE KITCHEN GARDEN WALL, the soft thunk of a spade slicing into well-turned earth can be heard, and the voice of the European hired gardener instructing his slave assistants. Smoke from a hickory and apple log fire seeps from the meat house, alerting us to the good hams and bacon curing within, Martha Washington's pride. Washington once explained to Lafayette, lover of American democracy, that "Virginia Ladies value themselves on the goodness of their bacon." Across the entrance-drive circle, the whir of the wheel and thud of the loom are proof that spinners and weavers are making some of the 1,200 yards of homespun cloth

Left: A LIGHT FROST

Hand-turned clods in the lower garden are tipped with frost as winter approaches. Clearing and spading soil in fall allows freezing and thawing to "work" the ground.

produced here in good years. Slave children, too young to work in the fields, have escaped their babysitter and are playing on the green grass of the entrance lawn, just where they are not supposed to be.

   Whoever is in charge of the household daily rounds, whether it's Martha Washington when she's home, or her niece, Fanny Bassett Washington, makes a chinking sound as she walks. It's the huge bunch of keys at her waist, which open all the places where household supplies are stored. Vital plantation supplies, such as salt or black-smith's files, are also stored and doled out as needed. Some have to be imported at

Above: MULES IN HARNESS

Washington was the first in this country to breed mules, crosses between donkeys and horses. He recognized that they were cheap to feed and willing workers, contrary to legend.

Right: BLUE FLAX FLOWERS

Linum usitatissimum *is the only species of flax that produces cloth but* **Linum perenne,** *seen here, is more gardenworthy.*

Opposite: THE SPINNING AND SALT HOUSES ON THE NORTH LANE

Ten or more slaves were constantly at work here, spinning and knitting homegrown flax and wool for blankets and clothing.

Below: GRAIN AND GRASS

An ear of wheat and Roque's Burnett, a fodder grass. From **The Complete Farmer** *(London, 1769 edition).*

great cost and take a long time to come from England. The steamy white smell of laundry in a big kettle in the washhouse boils out the open door, a welcome antidote to the dark whiff from one of the pair of octagonal privies, or "necessaries," set in the corners of the garden walls that are nearest the house. The walks to the privies are lined with sweet-smelling shrubs such as lilacs. Turkeys, geese, chickens, ducks, and guinea fowl strut, honk, chuckle, and shriek continually, especially at daybreak.

Depending on the time of year, the house steward, Frank Lee, may be gathering "Indian walnutts" to pickle, or a house slave or gardener gathering mint to distill mint water, good for the "cholick." When it flowers is the precise moment to pick it, writes Martha to Fanny, keeping a finger on the pulse of the seasons from the great distance of Philadelphia. In early fall, ripe white or black figs hide under their leaves, all the sweeter when sugar is a precious commodity. Returning at last to the house, we

Right: FIGS FROM THE LOWER GARDEN

Ficus carica, *'Brown Turkey' variety, ripened by the warmth of brick walls.*

Above: SYRINGA VULGARIS,
THE COMMON LILAC

"Removed two pretty large and full grown Lilacs to the No. [upper] garden gate," Washington noted in his diary for February 22, 1785.

hear the clink of china and the murmur of a tea party on the piazza. Shouts of Martha Washington's grandchildren mingle with the voices of visitors, whose accents are French, Dutch, Italian, and English, as well as Virginian and twangy coastal New England.

There were more than 400 visitors one year; some stayed only for dinner, but many spent the night. More than a hundred people were usually in residence in Washing-

Private Collection

Left: A TEA PARTY AT MOUNT VERNON

Benjamin Henry Latrobe's swift watercolor brush caught George Washington peering through his telescope and Martha at the teatable in July 1796. Nelly Custis, Martha's granddaughter, strikes an attitude. The others may be Tobias Lear, Washington's secretary, and Lear's son.

POACHED PEARS

The covered dish is part of the service of "blew and white China in common use."

ton's "rural village." His only unassailable privacy came in his study in the early morning hours, or on his horse, making his daily rounds of the 7,600 acres that comprised the five farms. By the 1770s, the "Home House," as Washington fondly called his dwelling, had become under his stewardship the heart and brains of a huge mixed farming enterprise.

O VER WASHINGTON'S LIFETIME, he planted more than sixty different crops and developed elaborate rotation systems to rest the soil. He was an admirable model farmer, though in the end he himself could see he was not a successful one, beaten finally by the stiff, infertile, clay soil and the population growth of his slaves. His experiments in the "new husbandry," the Enlightenment's scientific agriculture, were to be shared with the nation, an America that would become a "storehouse and

LIGHT ON THE RIVER ROAD

This puddled track has run along the Potomac below Mount Vernon at least since Washington rode along the banks of the river.

granary for the world." His own efforts showed the difficulties of world markets, however. He successfully left tobacco for mixed farming ten years before the Revolution, and then saw his profits slowly dwindle when the British West Indies market for grain and produce slammed shut against the United States after the war's conclusion.

Many seasonal routines are now carried out here at Mount Vernon that help recapture the original larger, intensely agricultural and self-sufficient flavor. At the raw, lifeless end of a Virginia winter — February — fruit trees are pruned so that they will bear more and better fruit. A little later, fields are plowed, either to plant with crops or to fold under a "green manure," some sort of winter cover crop that will fertilize and lighten the clay.

Within the brick walls of the upper and lower gardens, onion sets saved from the last season are planted out in March just the way they used to be, along with carrots, leeks, turnips, parsnips, and beets. Then it's time to put in kidney beans, peas, and more onions and carrots. The season of gathering is marked by the flowering of dogwood and redbud: now in the gardens there will be lettuce in April, strawberries in May, peas and a thousand-petaled burst of roses for rose water in June. The gardener will have "every thing in his garden that will be nessary in the House keeping way as vegetable is the best part of our living in the country," as Martha Washington wrote.

From the time the first seeds ripen until the end of November, it is a race with the birds to gather enough for the next year. Untidy squads of plants — Washington's domestic army — are left standing to set seed and dry. They give beds a different look from today's primly deadheaded borders. We begin to understand the beauty of decay as part of the cycle. Horse-drawn compost wagons below the kitchen garden wall are heaped with the frost-touched leftovers of autumn as the garden is put to sleep. In the newly rebuilt sixteen-sided treading barn — Washington's own thrifty and elegant invention — wheat is being trod by a couple of horses through the wide cracks in the boards. It falls to the granary below, heaps of gold in shafts of sunlight.

No sane person is going to build a sixteen-sided horse-powered threshing barn today, not even as a garden gazebo. But the gardening and design principles of Mount Vernon remain useful. Startlingly, so do many details of cultivation; their original rightness has been restored by the practice of environmentally sound gar-

Opposite: THE PATH TO THE SCHOOLHOUSE

*Every plant that produces seed will be left to stand in the upper garden until it ripens. These sturdy July bloomers are battalions of crimson beebalm (**Monarda didyma**), hollyhocks (**Alcea rosea**) climbing high past their bamboo stakes, and black-eyed Susans (**Rudbeckia hirta**).*

EARLY MAY

*Apples begin to set fruit on their cordons, top, and below, onions dwarf a tiny hedge of aromatic germander (**Teucrium chamaedrys**).*

dening. But more than anything else, it's the sense of personal involvement, almost of self-definition, in the act of creating a garden that Mount Vernon imparts to us. In "The Gift Outright," Robert Frost says it best:

> The land was ours before we were the land's.
> She was our land more than a hundred years
> Before we were her people. She was ours
> In Massachusetts, in Virginia,
> But we were England's, still colonials,
> Possessing what we still were unpossessed by,
> Possessed by what we now no more possessed.
> Something we were withholding made us weak
> Until we found out that it was ourselves
> We were withholding. . . .

Washington gave himself outright to the land, to its imaginative possibilities as a nation as well as to its bountifulness. Any piece of land that becomes a garden does so by the same sort of transformation. More powerful than mere possession of a garden is the daily act of being possessed by it.

CHAPTER TWO

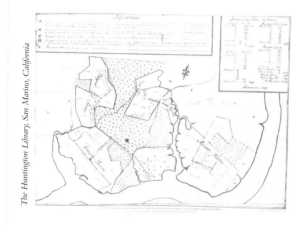

Making a Landscape: The Design

"The whole plantation, the garden, and the rest prove well

that a man born with natural taste may guess a beauty

without ever having seen its model."

JULIAN URSYN NIEMCEWICZ, 1798

WASHINGTON'S PLAN OF THE FIVE
MOUNT VERNON FARMS, 1793

*Any good farmer might have such intimate
knowledge of his land, but few could render it as
Washington did here, using his surveyor's skills.
The "Mansion House Farm" as he often called
the home farm, appears in the lower center, where
thinly dotted clumps of trees indicate its use as
parkland.*

Opposite: "HOME HOUSE" FLOATS
ON A SEA OF GREEN

*"The front by which we entered had a Gras plot
before it with a road round it for Carriages planted
on each side with a number of different kinds of
Trees," is how Lieutenant John Enys described
the recently completed bowling green in 1788.*

A GOOD SURVEYOR HAS TO HAVE THE EYE OF A SOARING BIRD, riding the thermals, scanning the land. It's a different way of seeing: the measurements confirm what's already known about the tilt and shape of terrain almost by instinct. That sense can't be trusted completely, of course — there are always surprises. But translation onto a page generally sets down a pattern for the ordinary person which already exists in the mind's eye of the surveyor. This is how it must have been for Washington, trained at the age of sixteen to measure and take stock of land.

The power to fly without leaving the ground would have taken him high above Mount Vernon in 1799, the last year of his life. By then it was an 7,600-acre plantation divided into five farms, with the 500 acres of the Home Farm used as a gentleman's park, leaving commercial crop production to the other properties. Washington, at sixty-seven, had been working his fields and shaping his landscape for forty-seven years. Its

THE WOODEN bowling green entrance gate at the brick ha-ha wall surrounding the pleasure grounds offers welcome and security, solidity and delicacy. The gateposts are sturdy, to stand wear and tear. Lighter palings and frame prevent sagging. Large ball finials herald the sturdy Georgian architecture of the house.

Washington designed the brick wall for the lower garden. He used a curve that follows the fall of the land and a pointed coping, or roof, which keeps moisture from seeping into the wall joints. If there is skilled labor and money available, a brick wall offers the best microclimate for early vegetables and tender fruit. Easy-to-make wooden grape trellises, seen behind, offer a visual division, inviting the eye to go beyond them. The posts are two-inch by two-inch cedar or white oak; the lathes are one-half-inch by two-and-one-half-inch cedar. "Six feet is the ideal span," says Theresa Keiser, Mount Vernon's head gardener, "because if it is longer, the lathes start to twist."

A "SNAKE" FENCE, a traditional colonial-period rail fence, was dreamed up when wood was plentiful. It can be built, dismantled, or moved quickly because it has no posts. The sharper the angle of the stacked rails, the stronger the fence. Other rails used as props, as in this photo, contribute to stability. The handsome but spiky irregular geometry of a snake fence also eats up space, so it is best used for fields and other rural locations. Cedar and locust are the preferred materials today.

WHITE-PAINTED POST-AND-BOARD is the dressiest, most expensive, and most labor-intensive type of wooden pasture fencing for large animals such as sheep, cows, and horses. Washington made sure the fence line along his stable drive was well whitewashed. Classic post-and-rail fencing, seen here behind the cedars, encloses the orchard below.

pattern was probably engraved on his heart. At the center of that map of the heart, though very much at the edge of the actual property, was "Home House," as he sometimes familiarly called Mount Vernon.

Around the clustered buildings the designs on the land were thicker, more evolved and symmetrical than anywhere else. As his mind's eye moved outward from the house, the patterns thinned and broke at last into less regular, more angular arrangements of orchards, fields, pastures, and woods.

WASHINGTON HAD FIRST KNOWN Mount Vernon briefly as a child of three, when his father moved to this piece of family property, then called Little Hunting Creek Plantation. After a couple of years, the family returned to the Fredericksburg area. Later it had belonged to Washington's elder half-brother, Lawrence, who named it Mount Vernon. Though it was also a family home, the plantation was laid out as a machine for producing tobacco for sale in England, like a hundred other midsized riverbank Virginia establishments of its period. The patterns on the ground that surrounded the main house had been very different then. When Washington became master of Mount Vernon, he transformed all of them — the gardens, circulation patterns, plantings, and field patterns — twice during his lifetime.

He first leased the plantation from his brother's widow, Anne, in 1754, but left it for the French and Indian War. When he returned four years later, he resigned his military commission, married Martha Custis in 1759 and settled in, inheriting the property outright in 1761 on the death of his sister-in-law. In preparation for his landscape works, he ordered from England in 1759 the solitary garden-design book in his library, Batty Langley's *New Principles of Gardening*, with its directions for laying out a country seat "after a more grand and rural manner" — the budding landscape garden. He would not utilize Langley's principles fully for another twenty years, but then Washington was always a deliberate man.

Those slowly completed changes in the landscape reflected changes in the man, his character, his political convictions, his vision of the nation. The upheaval that occurred in America during Washington's forty-seven years of gardening was mirrored in the embrace of the landscape garden as an acceptable form of garden art, even in a coun-

The two are used together to shape tall trees by lopping off unwanted branches. The long-handled chisel saved the gardener the trouble of climbing a ladder up to the branch: he placed the chisel at the bottom of the branch and hit the bottom of the chisel with the mallet. From **The Compleat Florist**, *by Louis Liger d'Auxerre, London, 1706.*

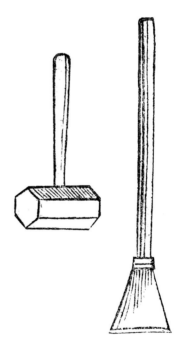

try where wilderness often seemed all too close at hand. Gardens have always been political animals, and none more so than the English landscape garden. To state it rather
too simply, the form had seen its beginnings following Cromwell's revolt against the
crown, which culminated briefly in the Commonwealth, and then the establishment
of the English Bill of Rights in 1689, which assured Parliament's power over the
king. In 1692, Sir William Temple, statesman and essayist, published his "Upon the
Gardens of Epicurius," which mentions the free style of Chinese gardens as a model.
In general, the powerful and popular association of individual rights and freedoms
with landscape was not made chiefly by gardeners but by philosophers and essayists
like Lord Shaftesbury and Joseph Addison. By the end of the first quarter of the
eighteenth century the Whig Party, who represented Parliament, the landed gentry, the
merchants, dissent, and reform, had publicly laid claim to the emerging landscape
garden as a symbol of freedom. It was characterized by what Alexander Pope called
a return to "the amiable Simplicity of unadorned Nature," by contrast with the old
geometric, axially symmetrical and topiary-filled garden, which came to be seen as
an embodiment of the aristocratic Tory Party and a symbol for authority and the royal
prerogative.

*I*N AMERICA THE POLITICAL TERRAIN, not to mention the natural landscape,
was different, and today's landscape historians, anthropologists, and archaeologists are still sifting out the course of garden history. Some hold that in the unset-
tled twenty years before the Revolutionary War the gentry elite of Maryland and
Virginia, many of them Tories, made gardens that were more controlled and symmetrical and therefore more traditionally English than ever before, as if they were
reasserting an authority that seemed under fire everywhere. Even given the considerable time lag in taste between sophisticated Britain and the provincial colonies,
perhaps for this reason it should be no surprise that Washington, a colonist but an English colonist, had felt satisfied at the time with his earlier design of the 1760s and 1770s,
which had been so clearly axial and pleasurably geometric.

Following the Revolutionary War, however, that same elite, now independent
Americans, tentatively embarked on a radical experiment in the redistribution of

political authority. The idea, so familiar to us now, was that all men are created equal, in a new world, free from artifice, where such a fresh start could be made. A larger polity was entitled to the pursuit of happiness, in theory at least. Nature "improved," in the form of a landscape garden like Mount Vernon's, was the radiant embodiment of those hopes for humanity's future in the New World.

*B*UT HOW CAN WE UNDERSTAND the development and import of this landscape design when what we see is the final result? Mount Vernon today is not only 200 years older, with all the grandeur and damages of growth upon it, but it also represents George Washington's most evolved landscape thinking in 1799. By the end of his days, he had joined a working farm, an arcadian landscape, and a business venture into a seamless whole.

Only archaeology and history can peel back the layers of soil and events. To start, it is necessary to get a view of that young man of twenty-six, back from the French and Indian War, walking and riding around Mount Vernon's acres, planning for wealth in the tobacco system and recognition as a gentleman of taste and decorum worthy to join the first ranks of the Virginia Colony. "I am now I believe fixd at this seat with an agreeable Consort for Life," he wrote in 1759, the year he married Martha Custis.

His first extended work at Mount Vernon was finished by the 1760s and coincided with the initial architectural renovation, which doubled the size of the house. The symmetrical geometry of the completed landscape set out a human order against the miles of forest that, at that date, lay only a couple of days' journey westward, above the falls of the Potomac.

Across what would later become the curvaceous bowling green, a straight drive led directly to the west door of a house much smaller and lower than it is now. The view was enriched by two flanking rectangular walled gardens and two pairs of highly visible outbuildings. Handsome and regular, though crude by the standards of the James River plantations Washington knew, this layout would also have been considered old-fashioned by English landscape gardeners in the 1760s. (In America by that date only a handful of American gardens could vaguely have been called "landscape gardens," that is, laid out either with unenclosed views, or assymetrically massed plant-

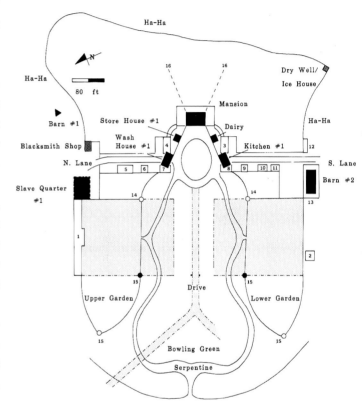

1 Slave Quarter #2/Greenhouse	9 Smoke House
2 Carpentry Shop	10 Wash House #2
3 Kitchen #2	11 Coach House
4 Servants Hall	12 Dung Repository
5 Spinning House	13 Barn #3
6 Salt House	14 Necessary
7 Gardener's Quarters	15 Garden Shed
8 Store House #2	16 Necessary ?

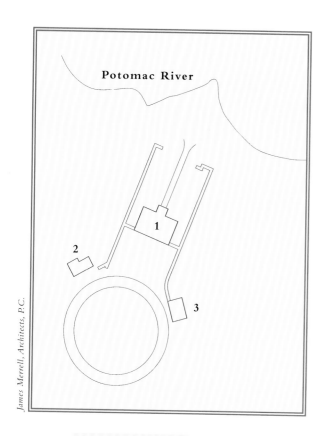

THE PLAN OF BELVOIR, VIRGINIA,
HOME OF THE FAIRFAX FAMILY

*1. Main House. 2. Office. 3. Kitchen.
The layout is similar to Mount Vernon's
first plan.*

ing, or sinuous design. Some few had been designed as early as the 1740s, such as those near Charleston, South Carolina, at Middleton Place, and Drayton Hall; almost all were made by men with close ties to England who were up to date on the latest fashions.)

Mount Vernon's first landscape — not yet really a landscape garden in the eighteenth-century English sense — was a portrait of the vigorous young George Washington, a man of the second-tier country gentry, not the aristocracy, trained to admire military orderliness and eager to make money as a tobacco planter. He loved luxury in clothes and furnishings and ran up large debts as a young man. For him "form" — including what materials he wore, or what silver or gold lace trimmed his hat — signified more than the pleasure of owning or wearing, just as the Piaget watch or Land Rover does today. But in his more stratified, less diverse society, the emblematic language of status and taste was more precise than now, when we assess the watch or the Land Rover but still don't quite know where to place the man. For Washington, a silver-laced hat or a long driveway directly signified his status to his peers. He was eager to become a ranking gentleman of the Virginia Colony and to have a place that signaled his position.

ECENT ARCHAEOLOGY offers a haunting and unexpected insight into the young George's character. Mount Vernon's first plan was startlingly similar to that of Belvoir, four miles downstream, the plantation of the Fairfax family, Washington's closest — and grandest — friends and neighbors, who were also connections by marriage. Washington's sister-in-law, Anne, was a daughter of Colonel William Fairfax. Fairfax, in turn, was the land agent for his cousin, Thomas, sixth Lord Fairfax, the proprietor of the Northern Neck of Virginia, a royal grant that comprised all the land between the Potomac and Rappahannock Rivers, or 5.3 million acres.

George had known Belvoir from childhood onward. His father, Augustine, died when George was eleven, and William Fairfax became one of the boy's substitute father figures, along with George's elder brother, Lawrence. But it was perhaps the Fairfaxes' version of English country life and the sense of culture, beauty, and ease it conveyed that made the deepest impression on the boy. And the kind of familial ac-

A MAP OF WASHINGTON'S VIRGINIA
NEIGHBORS

The young Washington's hometown world, the Northern Neck between the Potomac and Rappahannock Rivers, was bounded by both familial and political ties and connected by the water.

ceptance and recognition of his talents and character that the Fairfaxes accorded him must have stamped him too.

It was there, also, when he was sixteen and she eighteen, that he fell in love with Sarah Cary Fairfax, the bride of George William Fairfax, his friend and his sister-in-law's brother. Nothing except a few touchingly muffled, flirtatious letters seems to have come of their encounter, though Washington's romantic memory of her lasted a lifetime: in 1798, the year before his death, he would write more than politely to her,

LINDEN (*TILIA CORDATA*) IN FLOWER

Washington loved fragrant, flowering trees and celebrated his planting successes in his diary. On May 7, 1785, he noted that "The lime tree[s] which had some appearance of Budding when I went away are not withering . . ."

a widow living in England, that in his crowded life, "none of the important events . . . nor all of them together have been able to eradicate from my mind the recollection of those happy moments, the happiest in my life, which I have enjoyed in your company."

Thanks to the influence of the Fairfax family, one of the most powerful in Virginia, George met people who would advance his career, traveled abroad on his single trip out of the country, to Barbados, and was hired as a surveyor, all before he was twenty years old. So, with the private sweetness of friendship, family, long childhood memories, and young first love, and its public associations for him of power, money, advancement, order, decorum, and elegance, no wonder Belvoir seemed the ideal model for his own plantation.

Belvoir burned in 1783, but excavations have shown that on the approach side the visitor's view was sharply funneled by pairs of outbuildings connected by brick walls to each other and to the house. A forecourt filled the space between the outbuildings. The "funnel" was repeated on the other side of the house: the view toward the Potomac from the door was channeled by brick walls that terminated in what may have been privies. At Mount Vernon, Washington's treatment of the views east and west was almost exactly the same, with "running Walls for Pallisades" that connected the outbuildings to the house as well as to each other.

As is still the case with home improvers today, Washington's work was barely done before it started all over. The second phase of landscape began in 1774 and lasted until Washington left again for New York and the presidency in 1789. It coincided with his second and very ambitious architectural remodeling, which produced the present cupola-topped Mount Vernon. Work on both house and gardens continued during the Revolutionary War (1776-83) and was carried out in that eight-year absence according to his letters to his manager and cousin, Lund Washington, which often were written from battlefield encampments.

As he wrote, the contrast between his chaotic surroundings and his thoughts about a peaceful, reordered Mount Vernon was more than a welcome relief. He was also telling himself that the war would be won, Mount Vernon would not be burned by

c. 1735–58

1758–74

1774–99

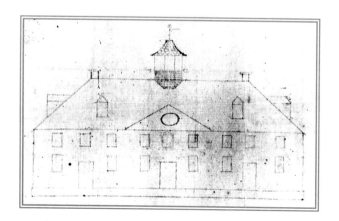

the British, and he would return home "to find," as he had predicted years before, in 1759, "more happiness in retirement than I ever experienc'd amidst a wide and bustling World."

We can't doubt that he meant what he said, even though eighteenth-century gentlemen routinely touted the virtues and pleasures of rural privacy over a public life in just this way, meanwhile advancing themselves politically, socially, and economically as fast as possible, as indeed Washington himself did for many decades. The language and the beliefs that it sprang from were part of upper-class culture, a graceful acknowledgment of literary retirees of classical antiquity, such as Pliny or Horace.

The historian Garry Wills has pointed out that Washington's efforts to retire from

"I T'S THE NICEST PATH underfoot — you relax when you feel it," says Dean Norton, the horticulturist at Mount Vernon, about crushed oystershell. He spreads it three-quarters of an inch thick on a compacted-earth bed cut to that depth. It keeps weeds down and does not roll or spread because it hardens to a firm surface with use and with rain. Crushed oystershell, also used for chicken feed, is available at rural feed stores.

"T URF PATHS are beautiful but they are high, high maintenance — they have to be both edged and mowed," says Dean, who is the thirty-fourth person in charge of the gardens at Mount Vernon. "And one thing they don't need is fertilizer — there is no reason to encourage them to grow!" He adds, "Any grass path you make should be wide enough for your mower, so it won't fall off the edge and scalp the ground."

N ATURALLY SMOOTH COBBLESTONES at the bowling-green entrance are worn even smoother by 200 years of wear. "Laying cobbles is a zen process," says Dean. "The beauty is finding the stones, then finding their flattest surfaces to face up — and part of the pleasure is their inconsistency. They don't have to match." Even a few feet of cobblestones gives a sense of timelessness.

E VERY PATH SHOULD BE CROWNED — higher in the middle — to help water run off to the sides. In his Mount Vernon brick kiln, George Washington made eight-inch by eight-inch brick pavers like these in his own little botanical garden. Good for high-traffic areas, brick pavers are also suitable for paths between buildings, since their large dimensions give a sense of matching scale. The bed here is crushed stone dust, which doesn't freeze and thaw as much as a sand bed.

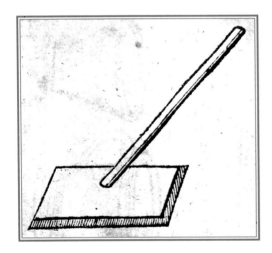

A BEETLE

This tool "serves to smooth Walks; and hinders
the growing of Weeds upon 'em. From The
Compleat Florist, London, 1706.*

public life were perhaps the most strenuous, heartfelt, and least successful efforts ever made by any American public figure. His second retirement — the first having been his retirement from the militia in 1758 before the end of the French and Indian War — was when he resumed a farmer's life, after the successful conclusion of the American Revolution in 1783. He said farewell to his officers in New York City in November and handed over his commission as commander in chief to Congress in Annapolis in early December. On Christmas Eve, he returned to Mount Vernon forever, or so he thought. That public act of renunciation transformed his rural retreat into a public stage.

"Power was acceptable only if those exercising it remained virtuous . . . and it could never be more than a temporary possession," writes the architectural historian Robert F. Dalzell Jr., adding, ". . . For Washington retirement was the quintessential republican act. But for it to have the desired effect, there had to be something compelling to retire to, which made Mount Vernon — and everything about it — all the more important. It was imperative that the house and grounds be kept in as impressive a state as possible at all times. And it was equally important that the place and its famous owner be accessible to any and all who might appear to see for themselves the great man living contentedly as a private citizen. Their reports to the world at large — of which there were to be many — would testify to America's (and Washington's) achievement of the full measure of republican virtue."

*I*T'S TEMPTING TO READ Mount Vernon's extensive 1780s "retirement" design as a metaphor for Washington's character. In fact, imagining the trip through his landscape to the house (before the entrance route was changed to accommodate today's crowds) even seems like a metaphor for the difficulties and pleasures of getting to know him. How appropriate it is to find that arriving at Mount Vernon's main entrance gate was not the easy suburban experience it is today. Isaac Weld, a visitor, wrote in 1797 that "very thick woods remain standing within four or five miles of the place; the roads through them are very bad, and so many of them cross one another in different directions, that it is a matter of very great difficulty to find out the right one."

MOUNT VERNON AT DAWN

A rooster crosses the road near what has always been called "the twelve-acre field." Roads and paths of all kinds were the primary basis of landscape design at Mount Vernon, first and foremost a working plantation.

*Washington, a military man as well as one
acutely conscious of social order, created a graceful
retaining brick wall and the entrance gates to the
bowling green. His masterful grading, which from
this viewpoint puts the house on a pedestal, raises
the visitor's anticipation.*

By the 1780s General Washington had become the secret George, the George who sat impassively still for his portraits, who was uneasily accustomed to being observed. A highly successful man of middle years, a statesman, he himself was well aware that he was a national icon, the "indispensable man," as one of his biographers, James Flexner, called him. His natural inclination to keep his own counsel had been strengthened by the intrigues and cabals of his war command. In retirement as determinedly polite as ever, Washington deflected talk of politics, policy, or the personal with his visitors.

ONCE THROUGH THE GATE the sweetness of the landscape as it unrolled across pastures and fields asserted itself, however. A curving drive swung off to the north from the gate, so that the house facade was glimpsed at the distance of a mile or so, and then hidden again by masses of trees. Washington's own undeniable sweetness of character was always a surprise to those who were initially taken aback by what his secretary, Tobias Lear, called "reserve and coldness" when he first started in the job. But Lear, completely won over several years later as he came to know his august employer, went on to describe how Washington "drew me towards him by every tender and endearing tie." As much as anything else, it seems to have been exactly that contrast between Washington's decidedly majestic, or "cold," initial self-presentation and his subsequent surprising humanity that struck most people who met him.

As the coach or horse trotted around the sharpish left turn to enter what were called in the eighteenth century the "pleasure grounds," the visitor got a real sense of Washington's open, almost childlike pleasure in ornament and invention. The sprightly cupola he had designed himself (slightly too small in scale according to some architectural-minded observers) sprang up above his new classical pediment. The curved drives flanking the bowling green of "about 100 paces" were backed by the brick walls of the two gardens, now also curved and set back — and topped with white picket fences, whose profiles were also curved. (It is as though Washington, being a thorough man, having once absorbed Batty Langley's idea that the curving line was the line of beauty, was determined to let no opportunity slip.) By 1789 the central bowling green was framed with several hundred trees and shrubs. The work build-

Sketch of General Washington,
by Benjamin Henry Latrobe, 1796

*"Washington has something uncommonly
majestic and commanding in his walk. . . .
His face is characterized, however, more by
intense and powerful thought, than by quick
and fiery conception. There is a mildness about
its expression. . . ." observed Latrobe about the
sixty-four-year-old Washington.*

ings and lanes had been swung away from the facade of the house, making of the working areas what many visitors called approvingly "a rural village" — the most truly picturesque feature at Mount Vernon.

The river-view landscape on the piazza side of the house was a totally resounding conclusion that, then and now, makes a sweeping contrast to the complexity of the approach. Washington's gestures, whether they were grand landscape effects like the piazza design or tiny domestic touches, were often more expressive than what he had to say.

Opposite: *A rural village*

*The plantation machinery powered by slaves became a landscape garden component: picturesque rooftops half-hidden by walls and feathery trees, like this black locust (**Robinia pseudoacacia**).*

Left: Perfect rhythm

*The sinuous line of the serpentine trees shows how thickly Washington planted. Here, the trees were on ten-foot centers. An old weeping boxwood (**Buxus sempervirens** 'Pendula'), probably a root sport of one of the plants given to Washington by Colonel Henry Lee Jr., stands at left.*

Right: The stable paddock and drive

According to many visitors' accounts, carriages often traversed this route to the house instead of using the serpentine drives. They passed the curving white paddock fence and the buttressed brick wall of the lower garden above it — signs of peace and plenty.

IN 1798, a young Polish visitor, Julian Niemcewicz, gave a surprising small detail of his idol's return to the house for dinner: "At two o'clock the General arrived on the back of a gray horse. He descended, shook hands, and gave a lash to his horse, which went alone to the stable." That playful flick of a riding crop (something every good rider carried but prided himself on not using) on the rump of a horse Washington knew would head off happily to his oats anyway, says a lot about control, custom, even affection. It also put a theatrical polish on the act of homecoming.

Similarly, the hieratic gestures typical of eighteenth-century portraiture — the hand on the sword pommel, the hand over the heart, the hero's turn of the head, with the eyes focused on the infinite future of middle distance — seem to have been invested with a more heroic cast by Washington. However limited his literary understanding of theatrical attitudes was, he didn't need to know more; he seems always to have known how to gather up emotion and subconscious meaning into gesture.

But perhaps his gestures had even more weight after the war. One of his biographers, James Flexner, concludes that the happiest years of Washington's life were between 1783 and 1789, when he left excitedly but a bit wearily for the presidency. After all, in returning to Mount Vernon in 1783, he had done more than retire: he

had behaved as he wished to behave; his private conduct had not been altered by the grinding circumstances of war. He had taken no pay but his expenses; he had held his divided forces together, gained independence for the colonies, and founded a new nation. His honor resplendent, he was highly sensible of the widespread love and admiration he had won along with the Revolution. Life's heroic endeavors were completed, and now he could plant his trees and finish creating his own symbol of independence, Mount Vernon.

N FACT, THE NEW DESIGN was still very much in progress when Washington returned in 1783. He oversaw its completion: the building of the conservatory and heavy planting not only on the bowling green but also on what was called the "West Lawn," the field west of the bowling green. The pleasure grounds were protected where needed by an invisible sunken brick-faced ditch or retaining wall cut into the slopes surrounding the house's high elevation. This ubiquitous eighteenth-century landscape feature, called a ha-ha, reportedly because it came as a surprise to a strolling visitor who would exclaim "ha-ha!" before falling into it, opened seemingly unfenced views but effectively prevented livestock from entering the pleasure grounds.

What ideal form was Washington working toward in all this? It's worth investigating what words like "beautiful" and "orderly" meant to him. Throughout most of his life, from 1748 when he went on his first surveying venture into the Shenandoah Valley and kept a journal of his experiences, the only beautiful landscape for him was a productive one. Though he and his contemporaries admired the natural landscape, they described it mainly in terms of soils and potential crops.

In 1770, he went prospecting for land in the Ohio valley. He was thirty-eight and had been farming and making his Mount Vernon landscape for sixteen years. As he came over the western ridge of the Alleghenies, he wrote, ". . . when we came down the Hill to the Plantation of Mr. Thos Gist, the Land appeard charming; that which lay level being as rich & black as anything coud possibly be. The more Hilly kind, tho of a different complexion must be good, as well from the crops it produces, as from the beautiful white Oaks that grows thereon. Tho white Oak in

A HA-HA

The section drawing shows a freestanding ha-ha constructed with a ditch and shrubbery screening. By following natural topography, Washington was able to sink his encircling ha-ha as a retaining wall because Mount Vernon stands on a rise. From **The Complete Farmer** *(London, 1793 edition).*

HEPATICA AMERICANA

The liverleaf, whose flowers are sometimes pink and sometimes blue, will colonize freely in well-drained woodland soil. Washington would have seen it on his plantation rides. From **Curtis' Botanical Magazine,** *Vol. 1, London, 1793.*

generl, indicates poor Land, yet this does not appear to be of that cold kind."

Because Washington is popularly presented as a sort of supremely practical super-farmer, we might think that he was alone among his educated peers in his emphasis on fertility in describing landscape. But even John Bartram, the Quaker farmer from Pennsylvania who became the greatest American plant collector, nurseryman, and botanist of his day, wrote about his explorations using the same language.

Redbud (Cercis canadensis) and tulip poplar (Liriodendron tulipifera) against the sky — a sight Washington would have enjoyed on his many miles in the wilderness. He planted both on the grounds at Mount Vernon.

On a trip north toward Oswego, New York, in July 1743, Bartram noted, ". . . After dinner we soon began to mount up a pretty steep hill, covered with oak, birch, ash, and higher up an abundance of chestnut and some hickory. This is middling land, the produce the same for three miles as our land bears with us. It lies very high, and when cleared will have an extensive prospect of fertile vales on all sides."

A hundred eighteenth-century explorers' accounts echo this tone. But the journals

of the next generation sound a new note: the beginnings of the Romantic consciousness. Although John Bartram's son, William, was writing in the same decade in which Washington traveled up the Ohio, the 1770s, his *Travels* are markedly different in tone. Exploring the Oconee Mountain in South Carolina he writes, "On approaching these shades, between the stately columns of the superb forest trees, [there was] presented to view, rushing from rocky precipices under the shade of the pensile hills, the unparalleled cascade of Falling Creek, rolling and leaping off the rocks from whence these delightful waters are hurried down with irresistible rapidity. I here seated myself on the moss-clad rocks, under the shade of spreading trees and floriferous fragrant shrubs, in full view of the cascades."

Pictorial, sensual, personal, conscious of self, and filled with visual expressions of movement, divorced from any thought of agricultural use — what could differ more from his father's sense of landscape, or Washington's? Washington was aware of that shift in perception, at least in the last two decades of his life. (One wonders if he hadn't read Joseph Addison's essays in *The Spectator* on "the Pleasures of the Imagination" and the "Beautiful Wildness of Nature," much earlier. They were first published in 1712 and then in 1744 as a collected set, which Washington owned.)

In Washington's later travel journals, though the old twinning of beauty and productivity still governs, there are hints of William Bartram's aesthetic understanding. During his presidency, he made five tours through the thirteen colonies, one north, one south. On a Sunday in April of 1791, he described what he saw traveling from New Bern to Wilmington, North Carolina, as ". . . the most barren country I ever beheld; especially in the parts nearest the latter; which is no other than a bed of white Sand. In places, however, before we came to these, if the ideas of poverty could be separated from the Land, the appearances of it are agreeable, resembling a lawn well covered with evergreens and a good verdure below from a broom or course grass which having sprung since the burning of the woods had a neat & handsome look especially as there were parts entirely open and others with ponds of water which contributed not a little to the beauty of the Scene." This is a different voice from the one that described the "Plantation of Mr. Thos Gist."

EAST FRONT OF MOUNT VERNON, ATTRIBUTED TO EDWARD SAVAGE, C. 1792

The brick ha-ha which winds down the hill, freeing the eye to look in all directions while invisibly fencing lawn from pasture, can be seen as a symbol of freedom — or as a metaphor for the concealed social distinctions that divided gentry from common folk. The division between free man and slave, however, was as plain as the white fences of the painting.

THE GREAT FALLS OF THE POTOMAC,
BY GEORGE BECK, 1796

*T*HIS NEW ROMANTIC, PICTORIAL UNDERSTANDING which, in Washington's case, is barely verbalized, is nonetheless quite visible in the changes at Mount Vernon, indoors and out. During the same period that he began to see landscape differently, he purchased paintings that were unlike anything he'd previously bought: picturesque American landscapes. The sublime found its place in two rugged views of the Great Falls and the Potomac in West Virginia by George Beck, 1796; the beautiful, in two pellucid scenes on the Hudson River by William Winstansley, 1793. He chose them himself (unlike the paintings and prints he'd had sent by job lot from

THE YOUNG UNITED STATES IN 1790

Seven years after the close of war, it was a national landscape still very much in formation.

England in earlier days), and they still hang where he placed them in the large new dining room, completed in 1787. As with the actual landscape, however, he didn't entirely abandon neoclassical symmetry: pairs of mirrors and Hepplewhite sideboards flank a military arrangement of side chairs beneath the Palladian window.

In speaking of his new landscaping endeavors, it would be easy to say that Washington was simply following fashionable taste or had observed the up-to-date gardens of Boston, Philadelphia, and New York, or that by 1790 Batty Langley's vision had become his vision. But Washington surely was too passionately involved in the evo-

**THE DEER PARK, A FEATURE OF THE
GRANDEST ENGLISH LANDSCAPE
GARDENS**

*"I have a fine 2 year old doe, perfectly tame, which
I beg your acceptance of. She shall be sent with the
orchard grass seed . . ." wrote William Fitzhugh
to Washington in 1785. Washington, who worried
that his steep riverbank would fall into the water,
might smile to see the timber retaining wall that
now keeps it in place.*

**WASHINGTON'S SKETCH FOR THE DEER
PARK WALL**

*". . . this wall is not to be laid out, or worked by
a line — the whole of it is serpentine," he wrote
to his manager James Anderson in 1798, imagining
his new creation from a distance and in amazing
detail. "It is not my wish to have it very serpentine
nor would I have it quite strait if I could — a little
curving and meandering would be my choice."*

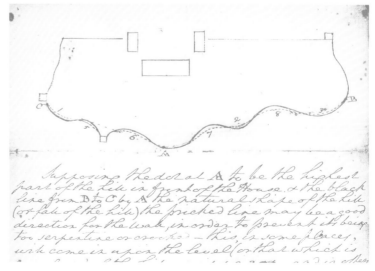

FROM THE CUPOLA TO THE WEST
ENTRANCE GATE

*After the Revolution, who was to govern?
Natural man, as free from artifice as from tyranny,
was the Enlightenment answer. In the New World
Americans would follow their own best nature into
wide-open westward prospects, like this view, or so
the thinking ran. In the new government, however,
the same elite that had previously governed the
colonies in fact reaffirmed its power. Laying out
landscapes by using geometry, whose laws were
natural law, conferred status, making a gentleman
out of a man, just as land ownership ensured
suffrage for the first half-century of American life.*

Below: REFLECTIONS IN THE CUPOLA
WINDOW

lution of his new nation not to feel the political reverberations of the landscape garden, however subliminally.

For Washington, the surveyor who soared over his nearly 8,000 acres in his mind's eye, the astute observer who could read the dignity of a hat, the emblematic meaning of his landscape garden must have been quite clear. Untrammeled by strict hedges or straight paths, with unfenced opportunity on every side yet created in harmony with nature's laws, surely this design was more than the design for a garden. It was a model of freedom, pleasure, beauty, and order for the nation he had fought for and founded.

CHAPTER THREE

Making a Landscape:
Plants for Vistas and Screens

"The blossom of the Red bud are just beginning to display.

The Dogwood blossom tho' out makes no figure yet:

being small and not very white. The flower of the Sassafras

was fully out and looked well."

GEORGE WASHINGTON

DIARY ENTRY, APRIL 26, 1785

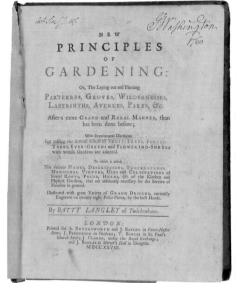

The Thomas Gilcrease Institute of American History and Art

O**N HIS DAILY RIDE AROUND THE FIVE FARMS,** W**ASHINGTON** never missed a chance to admire the woods and fields, and in 1785, he was especially intent on finding trees and shrubs to transplant. On April 26 he added a speculation about just how he was going to plant them: "An intermixture of this and red bud I conceive would look very pretty — the latter crowned with the for-mer or vice versa." Just so might we eye the balled-and-burlapped speci-mens in a favorite nursery.

Washington had begun to plant hundreds of trees and shrubs in front of his house in a day when there were few nurseries indeed on the en-tire continent of North America. Like his contemporaries, he dug sap-lings and young shrubs out of the woods; propagated cuttings; was

Opposite: APRIL FLOWERS

Dogwood, redbud, and a viburnum bloom together in the upper garden.

NEW PRINCIPLES OF GARDENING

Langley's book, published in 1728, was used by several generations of English and American gardeners because it offered not only design and horticultural advice, but also illustrations of planting designs. Washington did not take up Langley's more elaborate ideas for canals, basins, avenues, or statuary, however.

THE BOWLING GREEN FROM THE NORTH "WILDERNESS"

Age, and two centuries of care, have fulfilled Washington's landscape intentions of February 8, 1785, when he found he would be "very late in preparing my Walks and Shrubberies if I waited til the ground should be uncovered by the dissolution of the Snow," and so had it shoveled away to begin grading and planting some of the trees seen here.

given seeds, plants, and cuttings by friends and admirers, and had both plants and seeds shipped from England.

For the actual planting design he used not just his wild surroundings as a model, but also his knowledge of other Virginia plantations and his astute observation of gardens up and down the colonies during his eight-and-a-half years of wartime service. In Cambridge, Massachusetts, for example, he occupied a fine house on Brattle Street vacated by Major John Vassell, a Tory. The house had a forecourt planted with elms, a large formal garden, and views over the salt marshes to the Charles River.

He doubtless also reread his Batty Langley, that serviceable and chatty English guide to the landscape garden which he had purchased in 1759, twenty-five years before. The subtitle of Langley's book, *New Principles of Gardening*, written in 1728, neatly paraphrases Washington's own ornamental planting efforts at Mount Vernon: *The Laying out and Planting of Parterres, Groves, Wildernesses, Labyrinths, Avenues, Parks, etc. after a more Grand and Rural Manner, than has been done before.* A clue that Washington used the book is his use of Langley's terms to describe features of his new landscape: groves, wildernesses, and labyrinths.

WASHINGTON'S TWO MAIN LANDSCAPE EFFORTS were the river-front groves north and south of the house, and the 417-foot-long entrance-front bowling green fringed with trees and shrubs. The bowling-green plantings were started in 1785, following the groves, which were first set out in 1776. Each took years and successive replantings to achieve final form, mostly because of transplanting losses. Arranging in graceful groups, like designing the basic lines of the landscape, seems to have come naturally to Washington from the start, perhaps because he knew the growth habits of most of what he planted.

The groves framed the house from the river and screened off the lanes on the other side. The trees and shrubs around the bowling green framed the house as it suddenly reappeared after the long approach drive and screened the walled gardens and dependencies from immediate view. Of all the separate landscape plantings, the bowling-green ensemble is Washington's most ambitious effort.

ACCUSTOMED TO THINKING that what gets put in the ground will generally survive, we may find it hard to imagine the wholesale disasters that befell plants in the eighteenth century. What generally did them in was shipping time between digging and replanting, not to mention other practical difficulties, such as watering large plantings before the invention of the hose. The scale and speed of Washington's planting would have been impossible without the Home House work force and additional field hands pulled from the other farms for the "Waggonloads" of young trees.

Then too, eighteenth-century gardeners were planting experimentally in a way that is impossible to conceive of today: so many plants were new to them, and they had little or no cultivation instruction to go on. In 1786 Washington wrote to his child-

THE UPPER GARDEN AND THE CONSERVATORY

Edging box becomes hedging box over time and crowds the beds it was supposed to encircle. In the lower garden, onions, lower center, still find room.

hood friend, George William Fairfax, who moved to England before the Revolution, saying, "I will receive with pleasure and gratitude the seeds of any trees and shrubs wch. are not natives of this country, but reconcilable to the climate of it. . . ." He planted "palmetto royal" (*Sabal umbraculifera*) at either side of the west gate in 1785 and covered them that winter. But Mount Vernon, by today's zone maps, is in Zone 7 (average low temperature, 0° to 10°F); palmettos are hardy only to Zone 9 (average low temperature, 20° to 30°F). That's quite a gap.

Bad weather, as always, played its part too. In the spring of 1792, during his first term as president, when he was sixty years old, Washington ordered 106 trees and shrubs from the Kingsessing, Pennsylvania, nursery and botanic garden of John Bartram. Most died that summer in a fierce drought. In the fall, Washington wrote from Philadelphia to his superintendent, Anthony Whiting, telling him to expect 97 replacement specimens.

*D*ESPITE SUCH MASS LOSSES from time to time, and a survival rate that Washington himself once noted glumly as hovering occasionally at 50 percent, enough trees and shrubs eventually took hold at Mount Vernon to satisfy their eager planter's dreams. Some are there still.

An imposing boxwood (*Buxus sempervirens* 'pendula') with pendulous branches stands on the bowling green near the gate to the lower garden. Now nearly twenty feet tall, it is probably a rootstock scion, a survivor of a gift from "Light Horse Harry" Lee, Colonel Henry Lee Jr., of nearby Stratford Hall. In March 1785 Lee sent over the ancestors of the gnarled dwarf edging boxwood in the upper garden and ". . . twelve horsechestnuts, twelve box cuttings and twelve dwarf box cuttings." Washington's gardener doubtless nursed these in a sheltered place for a year before setting them out in their final positions, as is the usual practice with small rooted cuttings. In March 1786 Washington records planting the shrubberies with ". . . some of the slips of the Tree box. . . ."

While he was cooped up in Philadelphia in 1787, during the hot months of the Constitutional Convention, Washington visited Bartram's nursery (which still exists as a museum) for the first time. It was, Washington said, "stored with many curious plants, shrubs and trees, many of which are exotics," but he also noted that it was "not laid off with much taste nor was it large."

He visited the Prince Nurseries in Flushing, Long Island, during his first presidential term. Although it was famed for its fruit trees, which Washington admired, he wrote that it otherwise "did not answer my expectations. The shrubs were trifling, and the flowers not numerous."

CATALPA BIGNONIOIDES

The beautiful Southern catalpa, an American native also called the Indian bean tree, flowers in late May at Mount Vernon.

LIRIODENDRON TULIPIFERA IN EARLY LEAF

LIRIODENDRON TULIPIFERA IN EARLY LEAF

*One of the surviving pair of tulip poplars
planted by Washington on the bowling green.
In 1914, Charles Sprague Sargent, Director of
the Arnold Arboretum, assessed the health of the
remaining original specimens. He wrote (in 1926),
". . . no trees planted by man have the human
interest of the Mount Vernon trees. . . . No care
should be spared to preserve them. . . ."*

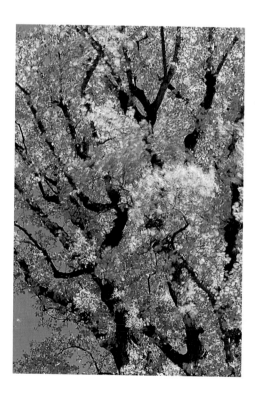

Both his brief comments amplify what he wanted at home. Within his overriding orderly design, his massed and banked thickets and plantations of trees both large and small, both deciduous and evergreen, were to be understoried with shrubs frothing with bloom and fragrance — "a perfect slope of beautiful flowers," as Langley directed. (When we say "flowers" today, we usually mean perennials, but Washington didn't, nor did Langley, who devoted exactly seven pages to flowers in a book nearly four hundred pages long.)

What Washington wanted was more baroquely crowded than a similar planting would be today, because of a difference in thinning practice as well as taste. The black locusts *(Robinia pseudoacacia)* in the north grove, for instance, were planted only fifteen feet apart, "thick enough," as he instructed his manager and cousin, Lund Washington, in December 1776, "for the limbs to Interlock when the Trees are grown. . . ." In the south grove, a space about 95 feet by 170 feet, in addition to more black locusts, he planted twenty-seven southern magnolias *(Magnolia grandiflora,* a tree he knew might reach eighty feet if it survived in Mount Vernon's climate), many weeping willows, and "the clever, or flowering, trees," that always held his eye.

Similar thick planting filled the long, narrow, curving areas between the serpentines and the garden walls, spilling over onto the bowling green itself at certain points and shading the drives, a protection from the Virginia sun we still enjoy today. The sections nearest the house were called "shrubberies." The westernmost ones were "wildernesses," a description that seems overstated, given the relative handkerchief size of the spaces — 108 feet wide at their widest points. But, since the beginnings of extended pleasure gardening in the Italian Renaissance, groups of ornamental trees had always been planted in regular patterns, such as quincunx and alley. When gardeners broke with that tradition in the seventeenth century to plant in slightly random order, they wanted the trees to look "wild," meaning, as Langley put it, "as if Nature had placed them there with her own hand."

The Vaughan plan shows a sort of all-over polka-dot planting pattern, neither geometric nor clumped in groups within the shrubberies and wildernesses. Thirteen survivor trees still indicate the shadowy framework of these

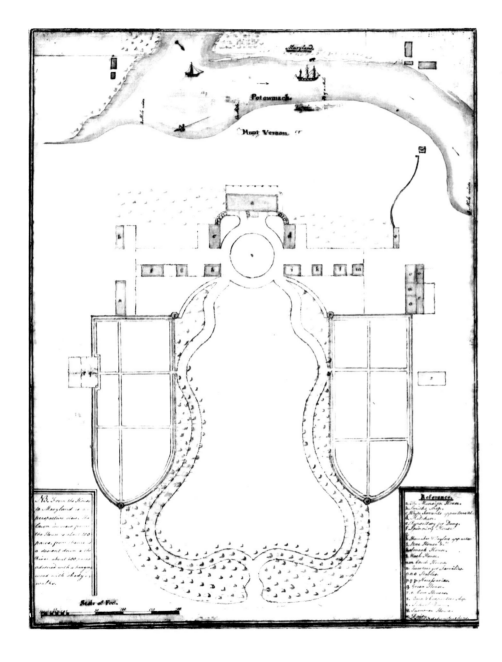

*The eye of the beholder is everything, probably
depending on how many landscape gardens
that eye has seen. Daringly irregular is how this
looked to the young Polish poet Julian Ursyn
Niemcewitcz, who visited in 1798. "The nearest
way is round and small [the forecourt circle]," he
reported, "the other [the serpentines] is large and
irregular. Many kinds of trees, shrubs, and plants
in flower adorned the two sides of the yard." To
Benjamin Latrobe, the architect and engineer, the
bowling-green area was a "level lawn bounded on
each side by a wide but extremely formal serpentine walk, shaded by weeping willows."*

THE FIGURE OF A SAW

From The Compleat Florist, London, 1706.

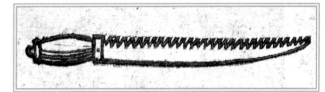

AESCULUS HIPPOCASTANUM

The white candles of a horse chestnut, another large flowering tree, brave a storm.

Opposite: ROSA EGLANTERIA

The pink-flowered sweetbriar, a wide-spreading species whose foliage smells like apples when crushed, was planted in Washington's shrubberies.

plantings. They include a massive pair of tulip poplars *(Liriodendron tulipifera)* along the serpentine drives; the one by the lower garden is 135 feet tall, with a girth of fourteen-and-a-half feet. To some visitors they looked irregular, but to us they look balanced, paired, as they did in June 1797 to Amariah Frost, who reported "rows of trees exactly corrisponding with each other" around the green. A large white mulberry *(Morus alba)* in the north wilderness shades the western end of the upper garden.

Vaughan's polka dots and various other records indicate that, between 1785 and 1788, 120 to 150 trees of different species were planted here, and who knows how many shrubs in these areas. They were spaced only about ten feet apart. Among them were southern magnolias *(Magnolia grandiflora)*; American hollies *(Ilex opaca)*; small flowering trees such as the native fringe tree *(Chionanthus virginicus)* and franklinia *(Franklinia alatamaha)*; large shrubs such as the native black haw *(Viburnum prunifolium)*, European guelder rose *(V. opulus)*, and Rose-of-Sharon *(Hibiscus syriacus)*; and American oddities such as the pawpaw tree *(Asiminia triloba)*. Fast-growing native scrub pine *(Pinus virginiana)* and the weeping and yellow willows *(Salix babylonica, S. alba* 'Vitellina')*, newly introduced into cultivation and very fashionable, were used as nurse trees to fill the gaps but were never intended to be permanent plantings.

When the major planting was done, and Washington had "levelled and smoothed" the green and sowed it with "English grass Seeds," he added, in 1786, two mounts, three-foot-tall turfed mounds of earth, topped with weeping willows at the western end. Mounts, unfashionable in England by the time Washington used them, act as a visual gateway to the western view, and their height allows the branches of the willows to weep still longer than their usual habit.

OF THE 105 ORNAMENTAL SHRUBS AND TREES mentioned by Washington in his writings (and listed in 1954 by Mount Vernon's then horticulturist, Robert Fisher), 62 are American natives. Of those, about 20 are species he mentions digging locally and replanting. Washington's journal entry for a January morning in 1785 describes the young trees of his farmscape and pastures that he wants to move: "Road to my Mill Swamp, where my Dogue run hands were at work [Dogue Run was one of the five farms], and to other places in search of the sort of Trees I shall want for

my walks, groves, and Wildernesses. . . . I found about half a dozn. young Elm trees . . . many thriving Ash trees . . . of proper size for transplanting, and a great abundance of the Red-bud of all sizes. . . . there are great abundance of the White Thorn (now full of the red Berries in clusters) [*Crataegus phaenopyrum*, our native Washington hawthorn]. Within the Meadow fence at the Mill . . . are some young Crab apple trees and young Pine trees in the old field of all sizes; and in the Branch of Hell hole betwn. the Gate and its mouth are a number of very fine Poplars, Locusts, Sassafras, and Dogwood, some Maple Trees on high ground, and 2 or 3 Shrubs (in wet ground) wch. I take to be of the Fringe tree."

Any gardener can recognize that Washington is already happily planting those "very fine Poplars, Locusts, Sassafras, and Dogwood" in his imagination. Since it is January and they are still dormant, he is going to have a go at spring transplanting. That was something he did a lot of that year, though a slow, muddy spring — "exceedingly miry and bad working" — bogged down the planting schedule.

*B*UT DESPITE THE MISHAPS detailed above, which all gardeners of the period endured, in fact Washington knew a lot about transplanting, its timing, its chances. He knew that deciduous trees could be planted bare root and that evergreens had to be moved with their roots undisturbed. Field-grown trees were better to transplant than specimens from the woods, because, he wrote to Lund Washington in 1782, "they have been more accustomed to bear drought and are hardier than those taken from the Woods, where sun, winds, frost, nor drought has had much power on them, and besides are handsomer."

He had observed what did well and what didn't — a real gardener. And perhaps as much as anything else, this love of trees, born of a familiarity with their nature and culture that was real, not literary or academic, was what gave him the extra push to make as naturalistic a garden as he did out of the formal elements of his old plantation.

He had learned to observe trees early. In 1748, at the age of sixteen, he took a trip westward into Virginia to the Shenandoah Valley frontier with George Fairfax and John Genn, the Fairfax family's chief surveyor. Washington was an apprentice on this

CORNUS FLORIDA

The dogwood, one of Washington's favorite trees, was transplanted from the woods and used everywhere at Mount Vernon. This old specimen flourishes its white bracts against the washhouse.

trip. "A Journal of my Journey over the Mountains began Fryday the 11th of March," he writes. The oaks and maples of the piedmont forest in March must have been fuzzed with their tan and red flowers. "Rode to his Lordships Quarter," he goes on, "about 4 Miles higher up the River we went through most beautiful Groves of Sugar Trees & spent the best part of the Day in admiring the Trees & richness of the Land."

As much as Washington loved trees, however, he also clearly loved the spaces between them, the vistas. His "prospects," as he called them, were so important to this polite man that, even in the midst of thanking Samuel Vaughan for his beautiful plan drawing, he corrected, painstakingly and firmly, Vaughan's major error concerning the view to the west.

In November 1787 Washington wrote, "The plan describes with accuracy the houses, walks, and shrubberries, etc., except in the front of the Lawn, west of the Ct. yard. There the plan differs from the original; in the former you have closed the prospect with trees along the walk to the gate; whereas in the latter the trees terminate with two mounds of earth on each side of which grow Weeping Willows leaving an open and full view of the distant woods. The mounds are sixty yards apart. I mention this, because it is the only departure from the origl."

Where did Washington learn about vistas and their importance? He must have gained much from his experience as a surveyor and as a horseman riding cross-country. But surely also he learned from his experience as a military commander. He was used to deploying troops over a landscape whose features — hills, bogs, rivers, woods — had to be grasped as a tactical whole. A life-or-death component of any battle plan is the way it offers through the terrain to the next place, either in victory or retreat. Such thinking is hardly the usual route to making a great garden vista, but it is tempting to think what urgency it might have given to a gardener who visually parsed a landscape in just this way almost all his adult life.

Every gardener is profoundly and even unconsciously informed — or should be — by the patterns of things he or she likes to do and is good at. It's part of what links gardening to everyday life. Washington loved to dance, for instance, an activity which in an age of set dances required an instant and visceral understanding of the

*". . . the best horseman of his age, and the most
graceful figure that could be seen on horseback,"
is how Thomas Jefferson described him. His
plantation round, his military service, his long
foxhunts — the rhythm and pace of life on
horseback was woven into his daily life.*

WASHINGTON'S SURVEYOR'S COMPASS

*He used this simple brass and polished-steel instru-
ment to lay out the grounds or measure his farm-
land, working with an assistant who would place a
pole on the position seen through the compass sights.
Surveyors use the same techniques to "take a sight"
today, though their instruments are more complex.*

marriage of pattern and music. First you went to the right, then to the left. No set of
steps was completed until that pairing was carried out. Washington had learned at
fifteen, paying three shillings ninepence to attend a dancing school.

Planting is a fundamentally personal act. Like dancing, it works best if the planter
works almost unconsciously, in a rhythm that pulls the whole together. For Washington, who knows how much the bilateral, echoing, mirroring pattern of dance surfaced
in the act of setting out his plantings in a balanced and symmetrical way, despite his
interest in the irregularity of the new landcape garden?

MORUS ALBA

A post and rail fence casts a late-afternoon shadow against the wide trunk of a white mulberry planted in Washington's lifetime.

M ANY OBSERVANT PEOPLE chronicled Washington's majesty of demeanor, noting also his solemnity and a shade of sadness. James Flexner, the Washington historian, says that "Washington's defense against melancholy remained movement. As soon as the initial exhaustion of war passed from him, he burst into multitudinous action. He assumed simultaneously the roles of expansive host, family and neighborhood patriarch, farmer, agricultural experimenter, landscape architect, interior decorator, merchandiser, landlord, exploiter of western lands, builder of roads and canals."

But, as if Washington were suffering from a kind of battle shock, Flexner adds, he seemed especially haunted by the thought of his own mortality in those postwar years of the 1780s when the revamping and planting of Mount Vernon were at their height. To the Chevalier de Chastellux he wrote, "Those trees which my hands have

One of the outstanding surviving trees from the last quarter of the eighteenth century, this ancient white mulberry stretches its limbs sixty-five feet in the air above the upper garden. Beyond the obvious pleasures of landscape, Washington cherished its deeper meanings. Contemplating the long life span of trees highlighted his own mortality, but it also promised him a continuity of living things on earth.

planted . . . by their rapid growth, at once indicate a knowledge of my declination and their disposition to spread their mantles over me before I go hence to return no more. For this, their gratitude, I will nurture them while I stay." He added that he came from "a short-lived family, and might soon expect to be entombed in the dreary mansions of my fathers. . . . But I will not repine: I have had my day."

It's a stretch to say a lifetime habit of constant activity and movement alone patterned Washington's planting plans, or that his conscious purpose in planting trees was to stave off melancholy and a sense of his own mortality, or to put the memory of war behind him. But knowing how he felt and what he thought at the time he was carrying out his plans surely illuminates Mount Vernon's special qualities as a landscape, chiefly a sense of grand and constant motion.

*A foal on the east lawn is improbable as fact —
the horses did not gallop over the lawns of Mount
Vernon — but is true to the spirit of Washington's
freewheeling landscape, and to that of the new free
land, the United States of America. Detail of an
engraving after William Birch.*

*T*HE PLACE LOOKS GOOD FROM EVERY ANGLE, and that's probably no accident. Within the web of larger views, such as that toward the river or back across the landscape of fields traversed to reach the house, there are many micro-vistas, expansions of fields of vision, alternations of shade and sun, glimpses of roofs, or gates, or peaceful pastures, or special botanical treasures. All are visual promises that don't fully deliver as destinations but instead contribute a constant enlivening flicker of delighted movement.

Mount Vernon's plantings play a large part in making it a landscape to travel through, not just a series of views seen from stationary points. It seems absurd to say that we can use any part of such a grand eighteenth-century design as this in our own small twentieth-century gardens, but it is just exactly Washington's method that we can use. Good planting demands wisdom about plants, of course, but it also requires movement through space, putting in a stake, looking at it, pulling it out, traveling past the spot yet again.

How much of what the secret George liked about landscape had been observed in motion, or *as* motion? All he had learned as a surveyor, as a soldier, a horseman — even as a dancer — aided him here. Flexner writes about Washington's eventual success as a military commander who learned from terrain and experience, not military theory.

He was an autodidact, Flexner says, whose "preeminence was achieved through a Darwinian adaptation to environment." His success ". . . was the triumph of a man who knows how to learn, not in the narrow sense of studying other people's conceptions, but in the transcendent sense of making a synthesis from the totality of experience." The same is true of his progress as a gardener.

VIEWED IN MOVEMENT

The double gates of the bowling green, glimpsed through a twin-trunked ash **(Fraxinus americana).**

CHAPTER FOUR

The Upper Garden

"... a neat flower garden laid out in squares, and boxed

with great precission. Along the north wall of this garden

is a plain greenhouse."

BENJAMIN HENRY LATROBE, 1796

HE TWO EQUAL, OGIVAL, BRICK-WALLED GARDENS THAT flank the bowling green in front of the house are something all visitors, past and present, make a beeline for in the Mount Vernon landscape. In Washington's day, the upper garden got a lot more press than the lower, especially after the brick conservatory was built in 1787.

The upper and lower gardens did not start off as a pair. By 1762 the rectangular brick-walled lower garden already existed, large enough to grow food for the household. The "new garden," which was in fact the present-day upper garden, must have been quite sketchy until 1776, because the encircling walls weren't finished until then. Washington kept moving fruit and nut trees into both spaces, both as standards and as espaliers, though he seems to have moved many more, and many more unusual ones, into the upper garden. He kept referring to the "new garden" as if it were an established place already, but in fact its shape was probably rather anomalous, like the reality of our own gardens, onto which we happily project visions of completion. It doubtless existed most clearly in his

Opposite: THE BOWLING-GREEN GATE INTO THE UPPER GARDEN

Sunset lights the posts, the palings, and the conservatory beyond.

MIDSUMMER PEARS

Washington grew eighteen different kinds of pears both for variety and to extend the season. Many of them were planted in the upper garden.

Spring

The schoolhouse, one of four identical octagons that are the focal points of the enclosed gardens, is reached by a path lined with bulbs in flower. When the plantings are still low, the curved beds are most visible. They repeat the curve that was the motif of Washington's overall landscape redesign, a curve also seen in the serpentines beyond the wall, the wall itself, and its swooping white pickets.

To keep crown imperial bulbs from rotting, plant them on their sides — a growing tip from Mount Vernon's present-day gardeners. Only species and cultivars mentioned by Washington, or known to be in common eighteenth-century use, like the fritillary, are grown here.

mind's eye, one of the things he wanted to complete as part of his symmetrical pattern of use and beauty.

But by 1776, the year the Revolution began, there they were, two solid rectangles filled with fruits, vegetables, herbs, and flowers. Their facing walls, topped with the same fancy little octagonal brick pepperpots seen today, stuck out into the sightlines of the old central-drive approach, which existed until the 1780s. Peace, order, ornament, the geometry that befits a gentleman — and plenty to eat — were the messages communicated by the visible presence of these gardens. The boughs of the fruit trees must have nodded above the walls, heavy with apples, peaches, pears, plums, cherries — a new Hesperides, in the new Fortunate Isles, America, where myths came true.

For all the documentation available in his diaries and letters, we'll probably never find out much about how Washington observed things, or how he adapted what he saw. He once said that though he knew there were rules of architecture, he was ignorant of them and used "no other guide but his eye to direct his choice." Who knows what "choices" he made in the Revolutionary War or as president; "Washington slept here" applies to beds in some of the colonies' finest houses, many with fashionable gardens and beautiful settings. Mount Vernon would have been on his mind. It always was. That surveyor's ability to see both the whole and its parts at once, mentally to superimpose a plan while walking through it, would have helped him see all the pieces fitted together: old, new, existing, proposed. Mount Vernon also would have held out to him the chance to make what he hoped the new nation would be also: an orderly, beautiful, and prosperous composition.

It seemed clear to him, when the arms of his plantation plan were swung wide during the late 1770s at the beginning of his second phase of landscape development, that the enclosed gardens would have to become invisible. This job was undertaken in 1785 when the inner walls of the rectangles, the ones that had jutted out into the old axial view, were dismantled and rebuilt differently. Washington was transforming a business machine — the plantation — into a machine for living, where the "machinery" operated more efficiently, but less visibly, more picturesquely.

HEMEROCALLIS FLAVA

*Washington would have recognized the yellow
daylily from familiarity with its orange cousin,*
Hemerocallis fulva, *which was brought to
this continent by early settlers. From* **Curtis'
Botanical Magazine,** *Vol. 1, London, 1793.*

Moving the gardens out of sight, so to speak, had both iconographic and practical consequences. The old visible and geometric enumeration of plantation order — the dependencies, the gardens, etc. — was relinquished in favor of a more subtle overall effect of peace and plenty. The pattern in his head was effectively a picturesque one where the curved line was Nature's gift, according to his guide, Batty Langley. So the ends of the new walls were curved to be in harmony with all the other new landscape curves, creating the ogival shapes. But by doing so, Washington sacrificed some space and efficiency of cultivation. Because he was a practical man, he made up for the lost space by stretching the lengths of the gardens westward, toward the entrance gate.

Moving the garden houses was quite an engineering project. On February 4, 1786, "having assembled the men from my plantations, I removed the garden houses which

were in the middle of the front walls to the extreme points of them. . . ." Washington's diary entry marks the completion of the new garden outlines. How many men did it take to lift the little octagons off their high brick foundation? What sort of skillful balancing act — perhaps on rollers made of logs — conveyed them about 150 feet to their new homes? They looked down on the new curvilinear areas within the points of the ogives where some fruit trees had already been set out the year before.

Whatever changes were made in design or planting, the gardens had to continue to be productive, both in the end result, and while the changes were being made — sort of like keeping the Brooklyn or Golden Gate Bridge open while repairing it. They still had to grow what was needed for the household. So the internal organization, especially that of the upper garden as far as we can tell, followed the same gradual path from handsome utility to useful beauty as the entire Home Farm did.

For many reasons, what kind of a garden it actually was seems cloudy to us. We're used to clear divisions: "formal garden," "flower garden," "kitchen garden." These are distinctions that the eighteenth century didn't always feel impelled to make. Furthermore, additions to the garden changed its character over time, like the imposing greenhouse, the boxwood edgings, now grown to hedges, and the fleur-de-lis dwarf boxwood parterre set in crushed oyster shell (a favorite paving anywhere near the coast in the eighteenth century). And visitors' descriptions differed not only because of Washington's alterations, but because of their own varied experiences with grand gardens, both in America and abroad. Finally, the requirements, definitions, and design of gardens themselves changed over the long years of Washington's tenure and afterward. A visitor after 1800 might well have described the upper garden as a flower garden — since "flower garden" then existed as an important type — while that description probably would not have occurred to a visitor of thirty years earlier.

Samuel Vaughan, the man who made the well-known landscape plan of Mount Vernon in 1787, describes both upper and lower gardens as kitchen gardens, at a time when flowers certainly were also being grown in the upper garden. But what evidently struck him were the "Brockley, collyflower, leaks," cabbage, peas, onions, beans,

Opposite: BALANCE IS EVERYTHING

When Washington moved two of the octagonal houses to the pointed ends of the gardens, his slaves had to hoist them up onto the new brick foundations. The highest one, for the seed house in the lower garden, peers down at the sheep in the paddock below.

Following page: THE BOXWOOD PARTERRE

A fleur-de-lis design, set in crushed oyster shell, is the most formal element of what in July 1799 the Reverend John E. Latta describes in his diary as a garden "very handsomely laid out in squares and flower knots" containing "a great variety of trees, flowers, and plants of foreign growth collected from almost every part of the world."

88 Washington's Gardens at Mount Vernon

Taking cuttings helps get air and sun into the center of the plant," says Mount Vernon head gardener, Theresa Keiser, "so reach inside where it is especially bushy. If you do it right, you can't see it's been done, but the plant will feel better." Dwarf edging boxwood, *Buxus sempervirens* 'Suffruticosa', is a snap to root outdoors as far north as Zone 5. Make a clean cut on a woody stem (remembering that the bigger the cut-

ting the slower it is to root). Measure your four fingers from the bottom of the cutting to the first leaves. Then strip all leaves from the stem, dip it in rooting compound, and tap off the excess.

"Mix sand with any commercial potting mix," says Mount Vernon's horticulturist, Dean Norton, "and you can use up to 50 percent because it helps cuttings root. Make sure the cutting is securely nestled into the medium, and pack it down firmly to get rid of air pockets." A slow but sure method for a solid rooting medium is to fill three-inch pots in winter with potting mix. (Mount Vernon sometimes uses very finely shredded bark, as here.) Let them stand to settle until July, the season for taking cuttings for outdoor growing, or till September for cuttings for the greenhouse. Filled pots should be solid enough so that when a cutting is inserted, a single tug won't pull it out. Grow in full shade, with plenty of water and good drainage.

Seven months later, the finished product is "a mini George Washington box," says Theresa. This size plant can be set out on four-inch centers as edging box. If you can't bear to wait that long, tap out the pot to peek: after thirty days there should be signs of root growth. Then replace in pot and be patient. Theresa says, "as long as it's holding its own above," meaning that the top is a healthy green, "there's hope for it down below."

beets, radishes, lettuce, and celery, all of which were grown there at some time. Doubtless they were not planted interspersed and decoratively, as Savoy cabbages are today, but in rows that could be hoed. Then too, maybe the flowers presented themselves to Vaughan as they might have to a maker of sweetmeats: as ingredients. Martha Washington's index of desserts (even with one page missing) lists recipes requiring fifteen different fruits and nuts that would have been homegrown. (Sweet oranges, lemons, and pineapples, as well as ginger and tamarind for chutneys, were imported from the West Indies). And there are seventeen herbs and flowers also listed which could have been planted in the upper garden (as they are again today), including roses, violets, marigolds, mint, angelica, and rosemary.

On the other hand, in October 1793 Winthrop Sargent noted there were "Kitchen and Flower Gardens abounding in much gay and varigated Foliage — [and] a capacious Green house upon the right Wing stored with valuable exotics lay in my passage, offering a high Gratification for some Serious hour of the Day." Perhaps there were just as many vegetables grown in the upper garden when Sargent wrote this as there had been six years earlier, but what he wanted to see were not peas and beans, but ornamental variety and evidence of scientific plant collecting, both increasingly popular subjects for gentlemen.

Sargent was the first to call it a "Flower Garden," and it was always described that

Opposite: DIGITALIS PURPUREA

Common foxglove came to Mount Vernon as a gift in 1787 as "a cure for the Dropsy," along with "seeds of the rocket double Larkspur." Both self-sow in the upper garden today.

Left: PRIMULA × POLYANTHA

Rust and gold primroses planted with spring bulbs, including the bold-striped tulip **'Keizerskroon'**.

Center: VALERIANA OFFICINALIS

Sweet-scented garden heliotrope will bloom all July.

Right: LYCHNIS CORONARIA

Rose campion stands out against **Rosa 'Celsiana'** *and oriental poppies in late May. After rose campion's flowers are gone, its beautiful gray architecture remains.*

Right: ROSA GALLICA 'VERSICOLOR'

Roses such as Rosa mundi were grown mainly to make rosewater, to be used for its fragrance in the house and in cooking.

Below: ECHINACEA PURPUREA

The native American coneflower, one of the few splashy late-summer colors in the eighteenth-century garden. From **Curtis' Botanical Magazine**, Vol. 1, London, 1793.

way in subsequent accounts until Washington's death. In the early preservation years, when the sale of bouquets "from Washington's garden at Mount Vernon" helped keep the place afloat, the upper garden became as monumentally floriferous and elaborate as any hero worshipper might have wanted, a floral portrait of a slightly stuffy but heroic figure. Even today, the first impression is of flowers, perhaps because their ornamental, almost ceremonial value seems appropriate for a formal enclosure in the garden of the Father of Our Country.

phate. Dig up the whole plant, then divide it by cutting with a sharp tool if necessary, or by separating it with your hands, as here.

"FEWER FLOWERS on a perennial clump generally means it's time to divide," says Mount Vernon head gardener, Theresa Keiser, about dividing hot-pink-flowered rose campion, *Lychnis coronaria* (Zone 4). The rule of thumb for when to divide is "midsummer and fall bloomers in spring, and spring and early summer bloomers in fall," she adds. Some, like rose campion, a midsummer bloomer, are sturdy enough to stand division in either season.

"DON'T FAIL TO PREPARE THE NEW SPOT before you dig up the old plants!" is Mount Vernon's advice. They advise working in compost and, depending on the pH of your soil, a pinch of superphos-

GARDENER MATTHEW Peterschmidt sets divisions in place in the upper garden, and he'll water them well. Mount Vernon's first frost date is October 18 to 24, and they recommend division no later than a month before frost, so that roots can get established. However, if you must divide later, mulch the new plants for winter protection and they should pull through.

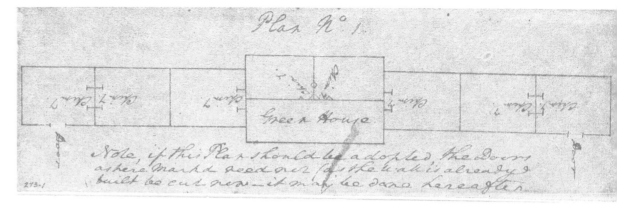

Plan Nº 1

Right: WASHINGTON'S *PLAN No.1*
FOR THE GREENHOUSE

*Washington's creative process occasionally
included trial drawings like this tentative
essay, the first for his conservatory, or orangery,
flanked by slave quarters. He also must have
made use of the many memories of architecture
and landscape collected during his wartime travels,
for in 1784 he wrote to get the exact details of
Mrs. Margaret Carroll's greenhouse at Mount
Clare, in Maryland, adjusting his measurements
and heating flues after receiving her reply.*

That first impression is easily dispelled: it is flowery, but that's not all. During the redesign of the upper garden in the 1980s, the old 40,000-bulb spring display was stripped down to a more appropriate size historically, and fruit trees were replanted throughout. Many, many roses still flower in June, but now, instead of recently introduced Chinas and teas, they are the six or seven deeply fragrant period roses that were used for making rose water and for cookery. (It took twelve days to pick the roses in Washington's time.) They have been redispersed in new square mixed beds instead of grouped separately in a formal rose garden. Right around the corner from the grand greenhouse and the pair of boxwood fleurs-de-lis are the rows of leeks and cabbages. Their frosty gray, or glaucous, foliage makes a nice contrast to rows of smaller dark green boxwoods, which are tidily lined up like a field crop to grow on until they are the right size to fill the gap in the edging somewhere.

THE GREENHOUSE, WARMED BY A HOT FLUE SYSTEM in the floor, and flanked by two slave quarters, was started in 1785 and finished in 1787. (The quarters were not completed until the 1790s.) But it wasn't furnished with appropriate plants until 1789. Then the plants arrived, gifts from Mrs. Margaret Carroll of Mount Clare in Baltimore to General Washington, after many polite, almost anguished letters between them. He begged her not to rob herself; she said her greenhouse was

overstocked anyway and it would cause her great distress if he didn't accept them. On October 29, 1789, Otho Williams, Mrs. Carroll's agent, sent "five boxes, and twenty small pots of trees, and young plants among which were two Shaddocks — one Lemon and one Orange, of from three to five feet in length; Nine small orange trees; nine lemons; One fine balm scented Shrub; Two potts of alloes, and some tufts of potted marjoram... on board the schooner Surprise... which sailed... for Alexandria."

Today, we admire the architecture and wonder how well the ingenious heating system of the greenhouse worked. We stare politely at the oranges on the orange trees. Their juice sits in waxed cartons in our refrigerators. Oranges are no longer the fruit of kings; possession of a greenhouse doesn't imply we have scaled the heights of power and fashion or that we have almost allegorical control over the natural universe, as it did in Washington's day.

Above: THE CONSERVATORY IN SUMMER

In warm weather tropical plants are carried or wheeled outdoors for decoration and color. At center left, a palm's topknot peeks over boxwoods. Washington first saw palms on his one trip out of the country to Barbados.

Opposite: INSIDE THE CONSERVATORY

Originally stocked with plants in 1789, the conservatory burned in 1835 and was rebuilt exactly, according to a sketch on an 1803 insurance policy.

Seed Collection

B LACK-EYED SUSAN, *Rudbeckia hirta* (Zone 4), blooms throughout July and August at Mount Vernon. Seeds are ripe when goldfinches arrive and seed cones blacken. Put the cones in a paper bag for a couple of weeks to dry, shaking often. This prevents mold and separates out the seed. (Mount Vernon's gardeners save some of last year's seed for identification for all seeds they sell.) Run seeds and remaining petals through a colander, then store seeds in a rubber-sealed glass jar in the refrigerator. Don't forget to label and date. Seed will germinate in one to two weeks in a greenhouse or under lights; it can also be sown in ground. "Black-eyed Susan is a short-lived plant — only about three years," says Mount Vernon head gardener, Theresa Keiser, so keeping seed is a good idea.

B LUE PERENNIAL FLAX, *Linum perenne* (Zone 7), blooms from mid-April to mid-May, seldom needs dividing, and makes a nice clump. Harvest when seed pods turn brown and begin to open, and follow the same process as for black-eyed Susan. Use a kitchen sieve, not a colander, as the dark brown seed is tiny. Flax seed will seldom germinate in ground from seed that drops from the plant; "maybe the seed is too tender to survive the winter here," says Theresa. It will germinate in two weeks in the greenhouse or under lights.

B LUE FALSE INDIGO, *Baptisia australis* (Zone 5), blooms from May 10 to June 10 at Mount Vernon. It stands four feet tall, carrying its clear blue flowers on sprays more than a foot long. "Don't despair if your plant looks spindly the first year or two," says Theresa. "It takes time to get established. And plant it where you want it — even a tiny piece in the ground will grow if you leave it behind when you move the plant." Harvest seeds after the beautiful seed pods turn black, but before they pop, as seeds will fly. Cut entire stalks with pods into a cardboard box, and let them dry — the cardboard will help dehumidification. Hard seed coats mean seeds must be soaked overnight in water; they will germinate in two to four weeks in the greenhouse or under lights.

S EEDS OF July-blooming biennial hollyhock, *Alcea rosea* (Zone 3), are ripe when pods turn brown and begin to open. Wear gloves if you collect lots of seed as their fuzzy coating irritates the skin. Cut the pods into a box and shake often to dry, or clean immediately and freeze the seed. They are prone to mildew and weevil, so if you store them in jars, add mothballs and two teaspoons of powdered milk wrapped tightly in paper towels to help dehumidify. Record the color when you label, and whether they're single or double. Barely cover seeds with soil as they need light to germinate, which will occur in ten to fourteen days.

How much more interesting to us than the oranges is what Washington did with some other planting boxes, which he describes in his diary entry for April 13, 1785. It reads: "Planted and sowed in boxes placed in front of the Green House the following things — Box No. 1 Partition No. 1 Six buck eye nuts, brought with me from the mouth of the Cheat River; they were much dried & shrivelled — but had been steeped 24 hours in water — Same Box partn. No. 2, Six acorns, wich I brought with me from the South Branch. These grew on a tree resembling the box Oak, but the cup which contained the Acorn, almost inclosed it;

BEANPOLES

Aristocratic boxwoods, tall and small, frame workaday bean teepees.

Washington experimented (unsuccessfully) with wine grapes in the vineyard enclosure, but he also grew table grapes in the gardens, like the ones just starting to wreathe the lathe fencing here.

Right: A FLOWER BASKET AND A GARDEN SIEVE

A fancy flower basket shows off the gardener's "genteel nature." With a sieve, "the Earth is reduc'd almost to Dust," good for sowing tiny seeds. From **The Compleat Florist**, *London, 1706.*

& was covered with a soft bur. . . . Box number 7 a Scarlet triangular berry the cover of which opens in 3 parts and looks well upon the Shrub." The plain box, the idea that he picked up something to plant everywhere he traveled, his hopefulness about those dried "buck eyes," his acute observation, all bring us close to him. The wooden box is also the kind of simple planting design we could adapt today.

The reconstructed design of the garden is not only truer to the original eighteenth-century layout but more appealing to our taste. It's much more casual, less groomed: we seize the swift seasonal round in the withered love-in-a-mist, left standing till its striped maroon seedcases ripen, or even the tall tattered stands of hollyhocks, waiting for their shiny little black coils of seed to spring open and be collected by the gardener for next year's sowing. Grapevines wreathing plain wooden frames make free-standing screens between sections of the garden; cherry and apple trees are neatly espaliered against the walls, as ornamental as they are useful.

The line between useful and ornamental gets crossed and recrossed, just the way we like it. Thank God we no longer have to complete our garden walks with gravel "taken from the nearest Pit . . . in a gully in the clover lot," which we have passed through "a wooden Sieve, to take out Stones of too large a size. . . ." But it may suddenly seem a good idea to grow leeks among peas, and peas among boxwoods — peasticks turn out to be surprisingly ornamental, and so do peavines. Or to have more raucous flowers, after seeing the shocking-pink plumes of love-lies-bleeding waving here. Or to collect seed for pass-alongs, or keep a garden diary, or even to see the plan of our gardens in our heads (before dropping another five dollars on another plant), the way George Washington did, the man who used his mind's eye.

Left: A NARROW BED

Daylilies and hollyhocks will bloom after the peonies and poppies go; the peony foliage will last till September, and the lamb's ears (Stachys byzantina) *add a valued note of gray.*

Above: ESPALIERED CHERRY IN FLOWER

Washington spent many hours grafting his own fruit trees as this 1775 memorandum shows: "On the 10th of March, when the cherry buds were a good deal swell'd, and the wite part of them beginning to appear, I grafted the following Cherries . . . 12 May Duke, 12 Black May, 6 Carnation, 6 May Cherry from Colo. Richd. Lee's . . . ."

THE HIDDEN UPPER GARDEN

Two redbuds and a red roof, glimpsed through the black shade of a southern magnolia (**Magnolia grandiflora**), *one of Washington's most prized trees.*

CHAPTER FIVE

The Lower Garden

"...I saw there for the first time preserved strawberries....

Those were large and beautiful, and I indulged in eating

a few of them. I have been fond of them ever since."

PETER STEPHEN DU PONCEAU,
VISITING MOUNT VERNON IN 1780

HROUGHOUT THE FORTY-FIVE YEARS THAT Washington lived at Mount Vernon, the lower garden was the place that probably changed the least in atmosphere and use, even though the walls were reshaped into their present ogival shape during Washington's second phase of landscaping in the 1780s. As far as we know — and we don't know much — neither the time-honored gardening techniques used nor the way the beds were laid out for convenience and good growth altered substantially.

On the other hand, the head gardeners, usually indentured Europeans, changed frequently. There were at least ten between 1762 and 1797, of many different nationalities. As well as gardening themselves, they were also supposed to know how to graft fruit trees, care for conservatory plants, and teach and oversee slaves detailed to work in the garden with them. When the Washingtons weren't home, the house staff was also supposed to help out. Even the exalted Frank, the steward, and Hercules, the cook, were expected to haul dung and help with the hedges.

ROMAN NECTARINE

Nectarines were only one of many "stone fruits," such as cherries, peaches, and plums, that Washington grew in the enclosed gardens. From **The Hot-House Gardener,** *by John Abercrombie, London, 1789.*

Opposite: IN THE MOUNT VERNON KITCHEN

Above the dessert delicacies — figs and nuts — and below the cascade of garden vegetables and fruits are squares of cornbread and a quart measure of grits. Cornmeal from the Dogue Run mill was also made into Washington's favorite breakfast, "three small mush cakes . . . swimming in butter and honey."

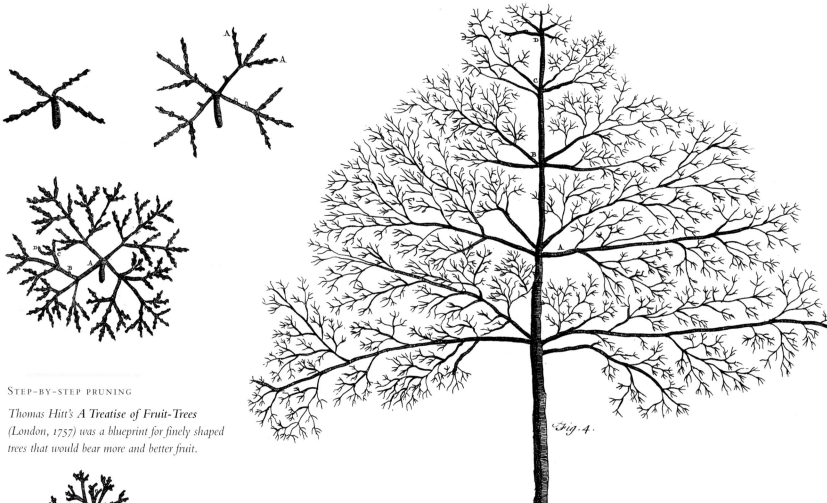

Fig. 4.

*Thomas Hitt's **A Treatise of Fruit-Trees** (London, 1757) was a blueprint for finely shaped trees that would bear more and better fruit.*

From the records, it's clear Washington had trouble finding the kind of head gardener he wanted. We can hear the voice of experience in a letter to his London agent in 1771, which runs, "I do not desire any of your fine fellows who will content themselves with Planning of Work, I want a Man that will labour hard, knowing at the same time how to keep a Garden in good Order and Sow Seed in their proper seasons in ground that he has prepard well for the reception of them."

By October 1783, Lund Washington, then the plantation manager, seemed to have become quite philosophical about the turnover and who was available. He writes to his cousin and boss about a gardener who had been hired in 1775, "As to Bateman, I have no expectation of his ever seeking another home. Indulge him but in getting drunk now and then, and he will be happy. He is the best kitchen gardener to be met with."

The gardeners' tasks were vital. "Daily bread," in eighteenth-century Virginia, was something produced at home every day of the year. The first requirement besides shelter at any homestead was "everything . . . nessary in the House keeping way," as Martha once wrote to her niece, Fanny, to urge the gardener on in her absence. In the lower garden, we know that vegetable staples and many fruits and nuts were being grown at least as early as 1760. That was the year before Washington gained clear title to the property. Perhaps that same spot had even been used as far back as George Washington's father's day, when little George was three.

BLACK WALNUTS ON A CREAMWARE PLATE

Nuts of all kinds gathered from trees on the plantation or in the woods were part of the Mount Vernon diet.

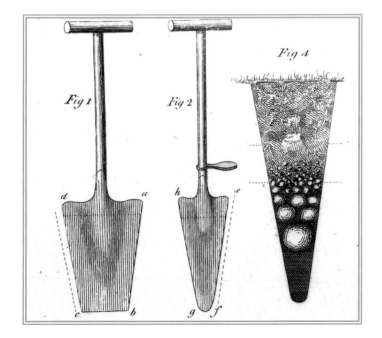

TWO SPADES

One for the first spit, the topsoil, the other, pointed one for the rocky subsoil. From **The Complete Farmer** *(London, 1793 edition).*

$\mathcal{C}$ERTAINLY NO GARDEN COULD BE BETTER SITUATED than this terraced spot facing southeast to catch all the best sun. Its sloping position tucked in below the bowling green means it enjoys good drainage and is protected to the north by the rise of the hill above it. The stables, a ready source of fertilizer, are right next door; the kitchen lies a few steps to the north; the seed house, one of the octagons, stands at the pointed western end of the garden, ready to receive the promise of next year's crops.

Washington completed the lower garden's first set of walls, the rectangular ones, by 1762. The combined two acres of both enclosed gardens produced a bounty for the family, the house slaves, and visitors. Even before he was a national hero, the numbers seem astonishing. In the seven years between 1768 and 1775 the Washingtons

THE EYE NATURALLY follows the path to what Washington called the schoolhouse, but what really makes order out of the happy chaos of the overflowing crescent beds in the upper garden is the brick edging. Upright bricks like these should be sunk at least two-thirds of their length for stability, leaving just enough above ground level to keep the gravel on the path and the earth in its place, under the plants. Pound the earth of the path bed down firmly before covering with gravel, to help secure the bricks.

BRICK EDGING, like this at left in the lower garden, can be sunk almost flush with a brick path. At far left is a row of green santolina, *Santolina rosmarinifolia* (Zone 6), another effective edging. Around the lettuce bed on three sides is a furry little hedge of wall germander, *Teucrium chamaedrys,* known as "poor man's box" (Zone 5). All edgings are tightly clipped to leave more room for food crops. (Kitchen usage would doubtless have kept herbs in their place in Washington's day.) Apple and pear cordons, dwarfed by constant pruning and shaping, are yet another edging.

HERB EDGINGS DOMINATE this corner of the lower garden, except for boxwoods rimming the horseradish at lower left and upper right. Common thyme, *Thymus vulgaris* (Zone 7), runs round the gray-green broccoli at center. Tarragon, *Artemisia dracunculus* (Zone 3), and sweet marjoram*, Origanum majorana* (Zone 7), an annual, enclose tiny lettuces at upper left, near the lilac-flowered chives, *Allium schoenoprasum* (Zone 5). Behind them are silver orbs of lavender cotton, *Santolina chamae-cyparissus* (Zone 6), another good edging plant.

PATTERNS OF BEANS, LETTUCE,
AND CABBAGE

"Tell the Gardener I shall expect everything that a Garden ought to produce, in the most ample manner," wrote Washington to his manager, William Pearce, in June 1797, the year he returned home from his second term.

TROPAEOLUM MAJUS

*The Mexican native, nasturtium, was grown at Mount Vernon. From **Curtis' Botanical Magazine**, Vol. 1, London, 1793.*

entertained about 2,000 guests; some were relations and friends, some were passersby put up at nightfall. After the war, as he wrote to his mother in 1786, he found the "absolute requirements of my family and the visitors who are constantly here are exceedingly high."

Washington was proud of his ability to take care of all who came, however, even if he complained about the weighty expense. He spent lavishly to furnish his dining table, the true emblem of hospitality in the eighteenth century. Its accoutrements — china, glass, and silver — were more elaborate than his furniture. After the Revolution, two cooks and two waiters, all under the direction of a house steward or house-keeper, stood ready to provide.

The Washingtons also helped the poor from their gardens and storehouses. Writ-

Left: THE LOWER GARDEN IN EARLY
MORNING MIST

*Low cordons of apples and pears line the paths
between beds of artichokes, onions, and lettuces.
In the background looms the stable.*

Above: STRAWBERRIES

*A straw mulch keeps weeds down, and the
berries stay clean as they ripen.*

ing from Cambridge in 1775, Washington told Lund Washington to "Let the Hospitality of the House, with respect to the poor, be kept up; Let no one go hungry away. If any of these kind of People should be in want of Corn, supply their necessities," though he added a typical thrifty and cautionary note, "provided it does not encourage them in idleness. . . ."

THE WEEKLY GARDENER'S REPORTS and Washington's diaries and letters tell us both what was grown and what the annual succession of tasks was for full-steam-ahead production of vegetables and fruits throughout the eight months of the growing season, and for the four months when the soil was "prepard well for the reception" of the next year's crops for the table.

The round began in the fall, with the clearing of the beds. Then came the manure spreading, which would keep up the fertility of the soil. "Wheeling dung [meaning compost] into the gardens," which extended through the winter and into early

Opposite: APPLE BLOSSOM

A CORDON OF APPLES

The ancient method of pruning and dwarfing fruit trees into low fences is both decorative and economical of space. These are hard-pruned when dormant and trimmed twice during the growing season.

CABBAGES

The colonies were at war, but the cabbages had to be planted. In his August 1776 account book Washington noted that in June he had bought "450 Cabbage Plants" and "250 Sallery Plants," as well as parsley, endive, and turnip seed.

SCARLET STRAWBERRY

*One of five hand-colored copperplate engravings from **The Hot-House Gardener**, John Abercrombie, London, 1789.*

spring, occupied as many as seventy-four man-days for the two to four slaves who worked in the gardens. Sowing began in early March with root vegetables and then peas and beans. By the end of March they were occupied with grafting fruit trees, spreading manure, digging artichokes, planting cabbage, and sowing cauliflower and celery. In April came asparagus; in May, strawberries were gathered; in late June, raspberries. Successive crops were planted in the same space, just as they are today: eggplant followed head lettuce; the last of the winter cabbage was followed by bush limas and then by a crop of fall spinach. (All the plants grown in the lower garden today are recorded in Washington's notes or in lists he's known to have used.)

There were one-of-a-kind projects as well: a beehive covered with a skep was built somewhere in the upper or lower garden, for example. And in June 1791 Washington made a note that "Frames for Hot beds [are] to be prepared for the Gardener according to his directions if it is not upon an expensive plan."

ON PAPER, MARTHA MAKES ONLY FLEETING APPEARANCES in the garden, though it is she who is generally thought to have supervised supplies for the kitchen and medicine chest. But it was often George who wrote out her requests for seeds and plants, or thanked those who sent them to her. Very few of her own letters survive; she may have kept a diary. Her situation is a classic one: women's domestic records of the period are few in any event, and those that existed were often thought not worth keeping until recently, with the emergence of women's history as a field of study. So how she orchestrated the complex delivery of, say, an entirely Mount Vernon–produced June dinner for eight of "a small roasted pigg, boiled leg of lamb, beef, peas, lettice, cucumbers, artichokes, etc., puddings, tarts, etc." does not survive. What lives on is only a unanimous agreement that she set an excellent table.

There is also slim documentary evidence in gardeners' accounts and other Mount Vernon sources for culinary or medicinal herbs, except for a single note about "digitalis as a cure for the dropsy," the parsley mentioned by a visitor as garnishing the cold breakfast meats, and the mint and roses that Martha was so anxious to have distilled into "waters." Rose water was also a common flavoring. The household copy of Philip Miller's *Gardeners Kalendar*, whose "LIST OF THE MEDICINAL PLANTS, which may

MARTHA DANDRIDGE CUSTIS WASHINGTON, AGE 65, BY JAMES PEALE, 1796

"The General was only a man, but Mrs. Washington was 'perfect,'" is how one of her dower slaves remembered her. From April of 1759, when she came to Mount Vernon, until her death in 1802, she had charge of the house, the kitchen, the spinning house and the washhouse, a revolving whirl of housekeeping, provisioning, cooking, sewing, and cleaning that she often handled from afar. (She spent the winters of the eight war years in campaign quarters, and the eight years of the presidency in Philadelphia and New York.)

Right: HERBS, FRESH AND DRIED

Martha Washington's charge included home remedies and household aids. The parsley in the scale was used as a garnish and described as a vegetable, but was also used in medicinal syrups. The pungent bay leaves at left, often used in meat cookery, were an ingredient in a Custis family recipe for a "sweet water," which freshened the stale air of a room when poured over a red-hot fire shovel.

Opposite: HOME COOKING CORNUCOPIA

Hours of gathering, chopping, and cooking would have gone into the vegetable soup at right, which might have included field-grown black-eyed peas at left. Cider, the most common eighteenth-century American drink, was served hot or cold, sweet or hard.

A CHEESE PRESS

From **The Complete Farmer** *(London, 1769 edition).*

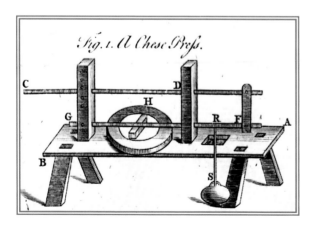

be gathered for Use in each Month" may have been consulted, as well as the list in Langley of "distilling and other physical herbs that are absolutely necessary." But we don't know that Martha, who would probably have been the one to look into the subject, read either of these books, although she had a library of her own.

The best guide to what herbs were grown in the gardens is probably the manuscript housekeeping book kept by Nelly Custis Lewis, Martha Washington's youngest granddaughter, who learned her housekeeping at her grandmother's side and whose home, Woodlawn Plantation, was staffed with slaves who had worked at Mount Vernon and been trained by Martha.

Two other sources are the cookbook Martha inherited from her first husband's family and a popular cookbook of the day, Hannah Glasse's *The Art of Cookery Made Plain and Easy,* which seems to have been used frequently.

From these we can gather she had on hand many herbs commonly used today as well as such oddities as alkanet (*Alkanna tinctoria*), a blue-flowered kind of bugloss that produces a red dye. It was used as an ingredient in her favorite lip balm recipe, from Hannah Glasse's cookbook.

THE CURRENT INTEREST IN HOMEOPATHIC and herbal medicine has made a commonplace of the idea that a plant can be both a culinary and a medicinal herb. Cooking staples such as onions and garlic were used medicinally, as were sage and all kinds of peppers. Garlic, for instance, used to flavor pease porridge, roast mutton, and a large meat pie known as a "Pasty Royall," was also an ingredient in a medicine made up by Martha to treat worms, then a common affliction.

Tying Down the Figs for Winter

FIGS, *Ficus carica,* can be grown as far north as Zone 6 with winter protection, and maybe even farther when grown against a south-facing wall, as they are here. At Mount Vernon, Charles Clements, gardener of the lower garden for thirty-six years, waits until leaf fall, after several frosts, usually around December 1 in Virginia. He prunes out dead wood and thins and tips his figs; then he sinks short wooden stakes in the ground near the plants.

"**T**HEN I LAY THE BRANCHES OVER and tie them down tight to the stakes," says Charlie, "otherwise the trees could die off and reduce the harvest for next year." Mount Vernon's figs are the hardy old-fashioned variety, 'Brown Turkey'. Home gardeners might also try some of the new Israeli hybrids, such as 'Schar Israel'.

CHARLIE MAKES HIS FIGS' WINTER BLANKETS out of straw. As it settles, he adds more. Rain will mat it down, he says, but an alternative to keep the straw from blowing would be to wet it down thoroughly, and even to cover it with burlap to keep the straw on the figs and not scattered all over the garden.

FIGS BEGIN TO SWELL IN JULY HEAT

RIBES SATIVUM

The common garden red currant, good for jellies and jams, puddings and fools, a dessert made with crushed, strained fruit and whipped cream.

Besides vegetables and herbs, soft fruit was grown in the enclosed gardens as well as tree fruits such as peaches and figs that thrived with extra protection. Apples and pears were also cordoned and espaliered there, but the bulk of the cider fruits were grown in orchards beyond, especially in the vineyard enclosure, which gradually became the principal orchard.

Young Julian Niemcewicz, visiting for twelve days in May of 1798 wrote, "In the evening G [General] Washington showed us round his garden. It is well cultivated, perfectly kept, and is quite in English style. All the vegetables indispensable for the kitchen were found there. Different kinds of berries — currants, raspberries, strawberries, gooseberries — a great quantity of peaches and cherries . . ."

Washington himself grafted and planted hundreds of fruit trees over the years. In the early years, friends and neighbors contributed treasured varieties to his infant orchards, like the grafts of "12 Bullock Hearts — (a large black May Cherry)" and the "12 Magnum Bonum Plums" from his neighbor, George Mason of Gunston Hall in 1760. As a young man he had learned to graft, and he must have loved it, he did so much of it. Every spring, until he went off to war in 1775, his March diary is filled with accounts of grafting cherries, peaches, apples, and plums on rootstocks he had planted. Often he must have used the quince rootstocks that Peter Collinson, the English Quaker plantsman, had recommended as good grafting stock to his "brother of the spade," the renowned Williamsburg gardener and Martha's former father-in-law, John Custis.

T HERE WERE OTHER PRODUCTIVE GARDENS besides the two big walled brick enclosures: slaves had patches near their cabins or on pieces of cleared land where they raised vegetables and "dung-hill fowls" to supplement their daily ration of a quart of cornmeal and five ounces of salt fish from the annual Potomac herring run. In 1792 Washington was clearing land down the hill toward the river, south of the house, about ten minutes from the slave quarters, "to give . . . a better appearance as the house [was] approached from the river." Since "the Home House people (the industrious part of them at least)," he continued, "might want ground for truck patches, they might, for this purpose cultivate what would be cleared." In this case, the view of

MAY DUKE CHERRY

Washington transplanted grafts of this cherry from his "Gardener's Nursery," the vineyard enclosure, into his gardens, both upper and lower. From **The Hot-House Gardener,** *London, 1789.*

cultivated ground, even of motley truck patches, was considered a pleasing one.

As for the design of the lower garden, it's very hard to imagine that Washington, the detail man, the man who believed that beauty and utility marched hand in hand, didn't notice or care about the design of the kitchen garden. However, we have few records by comparison with the detail available for, say, the bowling-green plantings. "Abundance" and "neatly laid out" seem to be the two things that visitors murmured as they made their tours. Vaughan's plan indicates square beds, though that may be just schematic rendering. There are entries for mowing the grass paths; many records of fruit trees, both as standards and as espaliers, trees "nailed" to the walls; records of a mint bed; and beds of artichokes and asparagus.

$\mathcal{A}$S IT IS LAID OUT NOW, the lower garden marks a significant period of American history, the Colonial Revival. It also charts the evolution of how the Mount Vernon Ladies' Association of the Union has viewed the duty given to it by Ann Pamela Cunningham, the founder, in 1874 when she retired, two years before the Centennial celebration of 1876. "Ladies, the home of Washington is in your charge — see to it that you keep it the home of Washington," she said. "Let no irreverent hand change it; no vandal hands desecrate it with the fingers of progress. Those who go to the home in which he lived and died wish to see in what he lived and died."

Although Washington's tomb at Mount Vernon remains a place of patriotic pilgrimage, today's visitors are more interested in every single detail of how he lived, thanks to the preservation movement, to the emergence of material culture as history, and to our own consumer interests.

When Mount Vernon was first opened to the public, the lower garden was kept closed; it was only after its redesign that it was opened in 1937. By then, the discovery that we did have an American history worthy of commemoration, a discovery that gained momentum after the Civil War and grew with the Centennial celebration of 1876, had produced the Colonial Revival. The movement was fully fledged by the time the Mount Vernon Ladies employed Morley Jeffers Williams, then a landscape architect teaching at Harvard, first to survey Mount Vernon in 1931 and then to "restore"

Opposite: OVER THE GARDEN WALL

*The built features, such as the dipping cisterns for watering, as well as the shapes of the beds, are taken from Batty Langley's **New Principles of Gardening** (1728) and other period sources.*

PLAN OF THE LOWER GARDEN

The landscape architect who restored the garden in the 1930s, Morley Jeffers Williams, followed usual Colonial Revival practice by making the design more elaborate than it doubtless had been in Washington's day. The patterns of the beds would have been simpler, perhaps a series of large squares as indicated on the Vaughan plan.

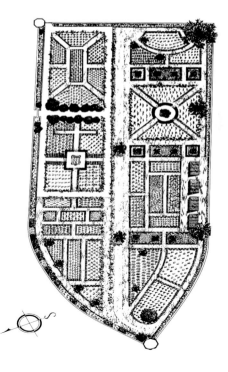

THE FIGURE OF A WHEELBARROW

From **The Compleat Florist**, *London, 1706.*

the lower garden. At its best, the Colonial Revival was the first attempt to honor American material culture — the architecture, art, furniture, silver, and clothing — by preserving the originals and replicating them for contemporary use. With the creation of Colonial Williamsburg in 1931, the effort extended to the patterns of daily life, not just the artifacts.

With the Colonial Revival, the carrots, peas, and onions of Washington's lower garden became iconic vegetables, symbols of what seemed, in the twenties and thirties, to have been a better, simpler, and more self-sufficient life, one to emulate. Unable to find actual documentary sources, unequipped with the kind of technology that allows archaeologists to study soil stains and phytoliths today, Colonial Revival garden designers and landscape architects turned to pattern books. To Morley Williams, by then Mount Vernon's official restorer, Batty Langley offered six very stately versions

LATE SUMMER IN THE LOWER GARDEN

A bed of purple chard is outlined with gray santolina, also called lavender cotton.

MOUNT VERNON,
JOACHIM FERDINAND RICHARDT, 1870

A detail of a post–Civil War rendering of a scene Richardt first painted in 1858 shows a steaming tray being carried from the kitchen to the dining room by a woman who had probably been born in slavery.

of the everyday kitchen garden, details of which, such as the dipping wells and the almost obsessively wide variety of herbs used as edging, were incorporated in the lower garden. This is the long way round to saying that the lower garden probably looked untidier in Washington's day than it does now, and that the patterns were simpler. Doubtless it was orderly, but it was not an ornamental potager like Villandry: half-picked rows, gaps in the cabbages, piles of litter, no august boxwoods to so delightfully obscure the entrance from the bowling green.

However, as we walk down the steps into the garden today, its overall impression is surely what it always was, a constantly changing but somehow unchanged map of plenty to look down on, striped with rows of dark soil and green vegetables, feathery with artichokes, a Washington family favorite, and in season always producing "an Abundance of Everything."

Above: CROOKNECK SQUASH

Ripe vegetables hide out under their leaves in late July.

Left: AN EIGHTEENTH-CENTURY CANTALOUPE

Washington's copy of John Abercrombie's **The Hot-House Gardener** *offers how-to instructions for pineapples in the greenhouse and "directions for raising MELONS and EARLY STRAWBERRIES." Homegrown fresh fruit was probably available eight months of the year, and was supplemented by apple and pear varieties that were "good keepers" in the root cellar.*

CHAPTER SIX

The Botanical Garden and the Vineyard Enclosure

"I am once more seated under my own Vine and Fig-tree,

and hope to spend the remainder of my days . . . in peaceful

retirement, making political pursuits yield to the more rational

amusement of cultivating the earth."

GEORGE WASHINGTON TO DR. JAMES ANDERSON,

APRIL 7, 1797

Opposite: THE BOTANICAL GARDEN

Between the salt house, at lower right, and the upper garden lies a small patch of ground that seems too humble to deserve the name "botanical garden." In fact, Washington often called it "my Little garden."

Above: A BEE SKEP

The Complete Farmer *(London, 1769 edition) gives full instructions as to "the Manner of raising BEES, and of acquiring large Quantities of WAX and HONEY, without destroying those laborious INSECTS."*

NO PLACES AT MOUNT VERNON BETTER SHOW OFF the secret George — his desire to be self-sufficient, his patience and his complaints, his enchanting curiosity, and his determined optimism, undented by considerable failure — than the botanical garden and the vineyard enclosure. Both places also lend weight to his status as an Enlightenment man who believed scientific experiment could improve the human lot.

Hidden between the upper garden and the north lane, in the shelter of the salt house and the spinning house, lies the little enclosed piece of ground where Washington probably spent more time gardening on

A SECRET SPOT

*Here, concealed by the curving garden wall, Washington sowed his experiments. They included nuts we know today, such as the pecan and the hickory, root crops for fodder like the oddly named mangel-wurzel, and even a crop of wild oats (**Avena fatua**) — alas, intended only for cattle.*

A SETTING STICK OR DIBBLE, WITH SEVERAL TEETH

*"It makes several holes . . . proper for the Sowing of Peas or Beans. . . ." Washington often experimented in the botanical garden with small quantities of different beans and peas. If they were successful, he would later plant them as crops in the vineyard enclosure or the fields. From **The Compleat Florist**, London, 1706.*

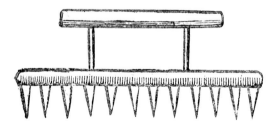

his own than anywhere else at Mount Vernon. He called it "my Little garden," or "my Botanick garden."

The first mention of it occurs in 1785 when on June 13 he "Sowed the following Nuts and Seeds, in the inclosure I had prepared for a Nursery, viz." and then listed ten different experiments, methodically "planted and sowed in Drills 12 inches apart." They included plants that would later be set out in the landscape, such as common privet (*Ligustrum vulgare*), which are still there, and household items he previously had had to purchase, such as what he called "Bird pepper" and "Cayan pepper"(*Capsicum sp.*) Others of these plants we don't see at Mount Vernon today, such as Pride of China or Chinaberry tree (*Melia azedarach*), which is too tender for Mount Vernon's climate but thrives all over the more southern South. He also planted seeds of the brightly colored tropical "flower fence," pride-of-Barbados (*Caesalpina pulcherrima*), "used in the West Indies . . . as an inclosure to Gardens."

Washington, like all intrepid, truly interested gardeners, had a real affinity for plants that were too tender for his climate. But in his case, we can legitimately wonder whether he was also pushed by a beautifully colored memory of his one trip out of the country, to Barbados with his dying brother, Lawrence, in 1751. ". . . the beautiful prospects which on every side presented to our view The fields of Cain, Corn, Fruit Trees &ca. in a delightful Green," was how he had described it in his diary at nineteen.

THE 1785 BOTANICAL GARDEN SOWING of flowering shrubs and other ornamentals, experimental hedging plants, nuts, fruits and seasonings, new grains and grasses, and a marked absence of either annual or perennial flowers, sums up Washington's experimental garden and farm interests and characterizes what he continued to try in the botanical garden for the rest of his life.

When he was home, he did the sowing himself. He marked the planting locations, often with notched sticks as substitutes for labels (number of notches duly noted in his diary for translation), watered and mulched, and he kept track on paper of the successes and failures, as he did for all his projects.

In his long absences, whether as commander in chief or president, his correspondence with his superintendent was filled with anxious notes saying, "Tell the Gardener he must plant the hiccory nuts in drills" or asking, "Does the last, and present years planting of Honey locust seed come up well, and is there any appearance of the Cedar berries, Furze seed, Lucern, &ca., &ca., coming up, and answering expectation?"

Occasionally there would be an outburst, as on February 1793: "Under cover of this letter you will receive . . . the white bent grass. . . . If the Acct. of it be just, it must be a valuable grass; I therefore desire it may be sowed in drills, and to the best advantage for the purpose of seed. These things which are intended for experiments . . . shd. never be put in fields or meadows . . . for there (if not forgot) they are neglected. . . . This has been the case of the Choricum (from Mr. Young) and a grass which sold for two Guineas a quart in England. . . . And the same, or some other fate equally as

ILEX OPACA

An ancient American holly on the bowling green, probably one of those started from seed by Washington in his "Little garden."

A HARROW FOR WEEDING HORSEBEANS

*From **The Complete Farmer** (London, 1769 edition).*

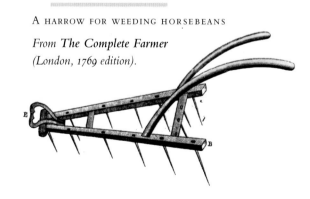

A GARDNER'S TRANSPLANTER AND
TWO GARDEN POTS

From **The Compleat Florist,** *London, 1706.*

bad has attended a great many curious seeds which have been given to, and sent home by me at different times but of which I have heard nothing more."

WASHINGTON'S INTEREST in growing better crops was not unique in his day, though he was renowned as a great farmer and many sought his advice. He traded seed constantly with his neighbors and with friends all over the eastern seaboard. In 1811, years after Washington's death, we find Thomas Jefferson writing, "With respect to field culture of vegetables for cattle ... we find the Jerusalem artichoke best for winter & the Succory [chicory, *Chichorium intybus*] for Summer use. This last was brought over from France to England by Arthur Young, as you will see in his travels thro' France [a book by Young], & some of the seed sent by him to Genl. Washington, who spared me a part of it." (In fact, the "Choricum" that Washington laments losing in 1793 is probably this same "Succory," so some of it did survive, though perhaps in Jefferson's fields, not Washington's.)

Washington's dozens of agricultural books helped him do research for the botanical garden experiments. The first work he bought on the subject was Thomas Hale's *A Compleat Body of Husbandry*, in four volumes. He possessed all the works of the standard authors, as well as many publications of the British Board of Agriculture, but in the 1780s and 1790s he relied chiefly for advice on his correspondence with Arthur Young, the English agronomist, who sent him not only chicory and other seeds, but also sent him his works as the volumes appeared. The back and forth of their correspondence is descriptive of customs in both their countries and analytical in the best vein of "the new husbandry," as Enlightenment agriculture came to be called.

The botanical garden was Washington's practical laboratory. His methodical search for agricultural ideas recalls what Richard Brookhiser, in *Founding Father*, identified as Washington's search for "right ideas about politics and government" and how he went about "the process of studying them and sharpening his understanding of them," which went on all his life.

A very good judge of character, Washington knew who to choose as his political mentors, beginning with his neighbor George Mason, in the decade before the Revolution. (Later, James Madison became his political confidant and was followed by

Alexander Hamilton.) During the long constitutional debates in 1787, Washington read not only the *Federalist* papers, but all the other published arguments, for and against. He devoured political pamphlets for forty years, says Brookhiser, a period when "the controversial political literature of North America . . . was of the highest order." His success as president is the measure of his intellectual understanding; without it, he could never have negotiated the tricky currents of those eight years as well as he did. And he was still reading ten newspapers in his final retirement, noted a visitor to Mount Vernon in the 1790s.

His agricultural experimentation, as James Flexner writes, was based on extensive reading of the English experts, but also on his unwillingness to accept anything on authority. He wanted to try it out in the climate and soils of his own country. (How familiar this sounds to modern gardeners who have learned that what goes in the Cotswolds often won't go here.) It has to be admitted that his scientific equipment was meager: he had a weather vane and a thermometer. The weather vane was as celebratory of the new nation's temper as it was indicative of the direction of the wind. An exact replica of the metal dove of peace made in 1787 in Philadelphia still flies over Mount Vernon's cupola with an olive branch in its mouth. And his methodology was quite unreliable: although he recorded the temperature daily, he often kept his thermometer indoors, which mostly tells us that the house was very cold. One winter day, he noted, "Thermometer at 52 in the Morning & 59 at Noon but removing it afterwards out of the room where the fire was . . . etc."

He was philosophic about his failures in the botanical garden, as elsewhere. Here, "at the very dawn of modern science," as Flexner says, Washington often ran controlled experiments. However, as Flexner also points out, Washington's recognition of how inconclusive his results were may well have been the best "indication of his potentialities as a scientist." In April 1786, he "Took the covering off the Plants in my Botanical Garden, and found none living of all those planted the 13th of June last, except some of the Acasee or Acacia, flower fence and privy [privet]. . . .Whether these plants are unfit for this climate, or whether covering and thereby hiding them entirely from the Sun the whole winter occasioned them to rot, I know not." Consistent with his character, of course he tried many of them again!

A FULL MOON THROUGH THE CUPOLA

Washington always noted the weather and sometimes the movements of the sun and moon in his journal.

Right: PLAN OF THE VINEYARD ENCLOSURE

Within its four acres Washington experimented on a larger scale with field crops and grew those vegetables needed in bigger quantities for the household. Over the years, it also became the most important orchard at Mount Vernon.

A STRAW BELL AND A GLASS BELL

The glass bell, or cloche, protects seeds "such as are sown in Beds immediately after the end of winter," and is still used today. The straw one would be useful today too, providing more circulation than the customary flower pot, which gardeners invert over a new transplant to protect it from the sun. From **The Compleat Florist**, *London, 1706.*

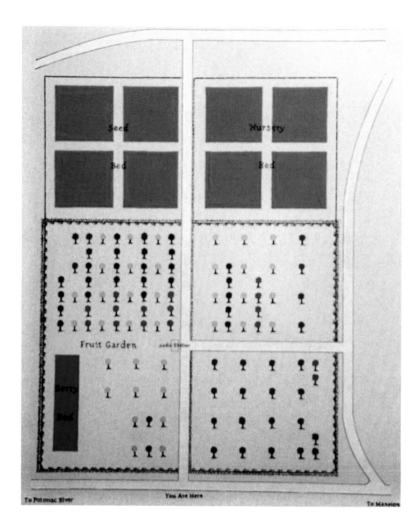

WASHINGTON WAS VERY CLEAR as to what the difference was between the botanical garden and the vineyard enclosure. "The intention of the little garden by the Salt house &ca., was to receive such things as required but a small space for their cultivation," he wrote in 1793. "And what is called the Vineyard Inclosure, was designed for other articles of experiment, or for seed which required still greater space before they were adopted upon a larger scale."

Restored today according to the most recent documentary and archaeological evidence, the vineyard enclosure grows not only useful plants but also ornamentals started as seedlings in the botanical garden which are still too small to set out.

AN APPLE CORDON GLITTERING WITH FROST

The four-acre vineyard enclosure on the wide south slope of the hill below the lower garden and the stable was indeed first used as a vineyard where Washington planted native and imported grapes in 1771. He never had much luck with them. By the 1780s, he was calling the spot a "Nursery," and trialing extensive quantities of grasses, grains, fodder crops, and peas (both for food and to plow into fields to improve the soil) that he had already experimented with in the botanical garden. Pumpkins were grown there, crops of potatoes and carrots and other "Kitchen vegitables of various kinds," and hedging plants, such as Scottish furze, whose seed he had first grown in the botanical garden as well. Honey locust, yellow willows, and many kinds of thorn, native and European, were other "living fence" alternatives. At least twice

LAGERSTROEMIA INDICA

A crapemyrtle in the shrubbery on the bowling green blooms best on its sunny side, facing the botanical garden enclosure. At bottom left are young southern magnolias **(Magnolia grandiflora)** *grown from seed as they were in Washington's day, as well as hot peppers* **(Capsicum** *spp.),* *far left, and feathery chinaberry tree saplings* **(Melia azedarach)** *at right.*

A FIGURE OF A TROWEL

A gardener "ought never to be without a trowel; by the use of which, he takes up Plants with the Earth about them, and without which . . . he would be oftentimes in danger of hurting them." From **The Compleat Florist,** *London, 1706.*

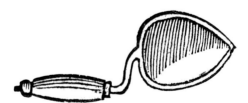

he imported white thorn (*Crataegus laevigata*) and must have had success with it, because after his death, 18,000 thorn plants for hedging (presumably still in field rows) were advertised for sale.

GRADUALLY THE VINEYARD, which has recently been redesigned and replanted according to the results of extensive archaeological and documentary study, also became "my Fruit Garden," the most important orchard at Mount Vernon. Four squares of sample trees were laid out: pears and cherries in one, peaches and apples in another, and two more squares just for apples. Somewhere at Mount Vernon Washington had nearly 300 trees of the "Maryland Red Strick," the apple Philip Miller recommended as the best cider apple in his *Gardener's Dictionary*, a copy of which was in Washington's library. The quantities seem extraordinary until we recall that both cider and peach brandy were made for sale. Since there was no refrigeration he grew nine kinds of cherries and eleven pears, which must have kept the season going as long as possible. Then too, though it's never mentioned, fruit must have been a special pleasure for a man with uncomfortable dentures and few or no teeth of his own for the last decades of his life.

Fruit trees and bushes were sent by Tobias Lear, Washington's secretary, to Mount Vernon in 1794 aboard the ship *Peggy*. Would George Washington please plant them, he asks in a letter, since he, Lear, doesn't yet have his own place — he'll take scions later. And please take some for yourself, whichever you desire, and give scions to your friends also. He sent gooseberries, the "Long Iron Coloured" and "Round hairy red"; unusual plums such as the 'Orlean' and the 'Seasmonna'; apples, currants, pears, cherries that Washington didn't have, such as the 'Amber Heart'; almonds, nectarines, and apricots. We don't know if they arrived, or if they were planted in the vineyard enclosure, but the idea that gardening is a pass-along venture shines through.

A portrait, even a self-portrait, of Washington still also shines from these two much-worked and much-loved spots of ground, and from the letters and accounts that tell their far-flung stories. More than plants grew up here: so did scientific interest; cheerful, unflagging hopes for a sprout or two; collegiality; and friendships.

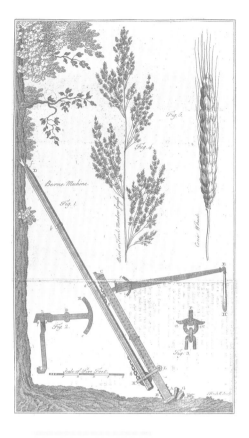

GRASS CROPS AND FARM TOOLS

Farm improvement came from the ground up, starting with the choice of fodder fed to livestock. From **The Complete Farmer** *(London, 1769 edition).*

ROYAL GEORGE PEACH

Surely a huge delicious fruit like this was worth waiting for. It took several years for the tiny saplings that Washington planted out to begin to bear. From **The Hot-House Gardener,** *London, 1789.*

CHAPTER SEVEN

A Storehouse and Granary for the World

"I think with you that the life of a Husbandman of all others

is the most delectable. It is honorable. It is amusing, and,

with judicious management, it is profitable."

GEORGE WASHINGTON TO ALEXANDER SPOTSWOOD,

FEBRUARY 13, 1788

FARMING WAS GEORGE WASHINGTON'S GREATEST pleasure; he also called it the occupation that "may be more conducive than almost any other to the happiness of mankind." Farming also amounted to a necessary obsession as he grew older. Especially after his return from the presidency in 1797 he continually pondered his balance sheets (almost always tippy) and how to improve his soil (bad), his slave work force (overloaded with those too old or young to work), organization (excellent — when he was at home), equipment (dazzlingly newfangled), livestock (greatly improved by breeding), and crops (he had tried more than sixty by the end of his life).

He also increasingly cared about how his farm acres looked, as if they were testimony to his own character, a mirror of himself. To be a good farmer ranked with being a good commander, or a man whose personal honor was unstained by cowardice or treachery. He seemed almost as

Opposite: HOG ISLAND SHEEP

An advocate of the "New Husbandry," Washington, who was interested in improving his livestock, bred imported English rams with his native-born ewes. Today at Mount Vernon, a flock of the same sheep from Hog Island, Virginia, his original native foundation stock, clouds the air with frozen breath on a December morning.

Above: FENCE POSTS LASHED WITH ROPE

Washington utilized animal droppings as fertilizer whenever he could; stock was pastured in harvested fields to eat the gleanings, and temporary fences, such as these, were used to keep them there.

TURKEYS AGAIN RUN WILD AT MOUNT VERNON

distressed by the news that his Potomac fishing operation had produced some bad barrels of salted herring as he was by the report of any political cabal against him. As much as he cared about his clothes, ordering in 1798 a fabulous new commander in chief's uniform of blue, "with yellow buttons and gold epaulettes (each having three stars) . . . and embroidered on the cape, cuffs, and pockets," he cared about how his hedges looked. He considered that they not only kept rooting hogs in bounds, but were "ornamental to the Farm and reputable to the Farmer."

He wrote to his manager, William Pearce, on October 6, 1793, "I shall begrudge no reasonable expense that will contribute to the improvement & neatness of my Farms, for nothing pleases me better than to see them in good order, and everything trim, handsome & thriving about them; nor nothing hurts me more than to find them otherwise."

*I*N THE SCHEME OF HIS LIFE, farming was the foundation in every sense of the word. It was, of course, the financial foundation. The bulwark of the war years (1775–83), when Washington took no pay, directed his affairs by letter from afar, left Mount Vernon's management to others, and saw his profits sink to nothing, was the fortune he had amassed in the previous fourteen years of astute, laborious land acquisition and management.

The structure of farming's daily and seasonal order also contributed to his thought process. Thomas Jefferson once described Washington's habit of minutely recording what he had just observed in his fields as occupying the time that another man might have used for reading. Washington was probably never happier than when he was setting down the details of each field gang's day, or when he had heard about or dreamed up a new way to fertilize his soil or thresh his grain. Like the air and rhythms of outdoor exercise, which he himself knew were an absolute requirement for his health, his reiterations of farm order and the receipt of his regular weekly accounts from the farm managers and overseers helped keep his habitual anxiety at bay. His hard work and good organization had been effective in winning what seemed an unwinnable war. Surely they would be as effective on the farm? They were a way of reassuring himself that he was in control of his life.

In 1754, WHEN HE BEGAN AT MOUNT VERNON, he would never have called himself a "farmer." He was a planter who, in the eighteenth-century Virginia sense of the word, planted one crop — that was his cash "plantation." A farmer grew many crops and sold in many markets, as Washington began successfully to do from 1765 on. For him, as for others, the problems of living off tobacco (an unstable market, all purchasing decisions and credit in the hands of a distant agent, many taxes) had underlined the larger difficulties of the colonial relationship with Britain, making, by the end of the 1760s, political independence seem only a step away from economic independence. (Interestingly, 1765 was also the year of the Stamp Act, the legislation that helped precipitate the Revolution.)

Wheat became Washington's biggest cash crop. His market output jumped from 257 bushels in 1764 to 6,241 in 1769. In 1792, Edward Thornton, secretary to the

A BUTTER CHURN

Enlightenment improvements hit even the housewife: instead of a vertical churn with a dasher, she could use a handy horizontal version with a crank and a stand. From **The Complete Farmer** *(London, 1769 edition).*

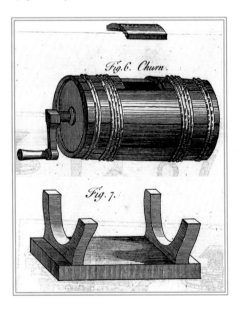

British Minister in the United States, reported an expected yield of 9,000 bushels, adding, "you will allow he is a farmer of no contemptible scale." In bad crop years, however, wheat profits were matched by what he earned on salted herring from his fisheries on the Potomac, which often yielded more than a million fish. Especially during the trade embargos before the war, and in the war years, he also produced goods — such as cloth from wool and flax for slave clothing — that he had previously purchased in England and bought seed — especially new kinds of grass seed — whenever possible from Philadelphia sources.

He had started with 2,126 acres in 1754, renting from his sister-in-law. The wardship of the Custis children and their 18,000 acres of prime tobacco land near Williamsburg that came to him with his marriage to Martha in 1759 helped him move up the economic ladder by giving him access to credit from the Custises' English agent, Robert Cary. Washington increased his Mount Vernon acreage to 5,500 by 1764, and by the 1790s his total acreage of 7,600 was divided into five farms, with 3,260 acres all told in cultivation on four of the farms, excluding the home property. The remainder was in pasture and woodland.

*D*URING THE SAME YEARS he also acquired more slaves, the unwilling machinery of his farm. He had inherited thirty-six and bought fifty more between 1752 and 1773. Martha had inherited eighty-four slaves from her first husband; among them were those who first staffed the house — about twelve people. In 1786 the first slave census was taken, a total of 216. By 1799 the slave population had increased by a startling 50 percent to 316. Why?

Washington had no repugnance about buying or selling slaves until he returned from the war, a war in which he had seen African-American soldiers fight as well as anyone else for ideals entirely at odds with the institution of slavery. In 1785 he wrote to his old friend George William Fairfax, who had decamped for England, that he never rode through his plantation "without seeing something which makes me regret having [continued] so long in the ruinous mode of farming which we are in." From the general tenor of his private correspondence over the next decade, it's clear he wasn't thinking only of the soil.

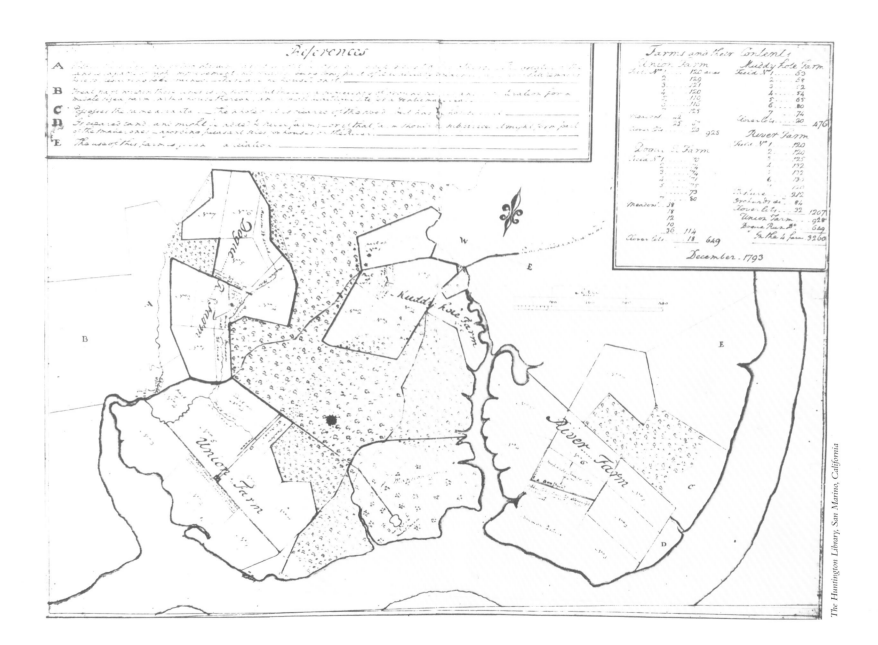

In the left column are listed his own slaves, those he could legally set free, and in the right, the dower slaves belonging to Martha Washington. Many of the Mount Vernon workers were skilled craftsmen and farmers: carpenters, fishermen, gardeners, hunters of game, cooks, stockmen, spinners, seamstresses, blacksmiths. Washington had made strenuous efforts to train his slaves, both to increase his own profitability and to prepare them for emancipation after his death by the terms of his will.

THE FIGURE OF A HOOK

This little sickle came in handy for "A Gardner that has Rows of Greens to dress. . . ." From The Compleat Florist, *London, 1706.*

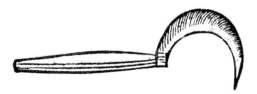

His attitude toward people as property had altered since the 1760s. In a private letter of 1793 to his long-time secretary, the faithful Tobias Lear, he wrote how much he wished "to liberate a certain species of property which I possess very repugnantly to my feelings . . ." While he was privately an abolitionist who wished "from my soul that the Legislative of this State could see the policy of a gradual Abolition of Slavery," publicly he was neutral, kept silent by his overriding desire not to shake the newly formed union he had fought so hard to establish. Apologists and critics alike agree that his balancing act became more and more difficult for him and was resolved only by his own death, when by the terms of his will he freed all his slaves, though he was legally unable to free his widow's.

His dilemma in the 1790s was economic as well as moral, largely because of the population explosion. He ranked among the top two dozen slaveholders in the Chesapeake area in the 1780s and 1790s. (Most Virginia slaveholders, contrary to myth, were middle class and owned two or three slaves to farm about a hundred acres.) But 42 percent of the 316 were too old or too young to work, or disabled. Furthermore, from the late 1760s onward, after he switched from tobacco to other crops, even without natural increase, his work force was too large for the job at hand. Tobacco took many hands to bring to sale; wheat and other grain crops and livestock care required many fewer. In the 1780s and 1790s, his postwar resolve not to break up families by selling slaves kept him still further away from balancing his plantation economy.

In 1793 he quietly advertised four of the five farms for long-term rent (saving the Home Farm for himself), first through a letter to the English agronomist Arthur Young, and then by means of newspaper advertisements and handbills. Washington's hope was that substantial English settlers might bring English yeoman farmers with them, to replace slave labor. There were no takers; one English farmer did make the long transatlantic trip to Mount Vernon, at Washington's expense, but decided the land was too poor to be farmed profitably.

To Washington, it was unthinkable — and would have been ruinous — to give up his lifetime occupation, which would have been the inevitable result of freeing his slaves during his lifetime. Selling slaves had become morally out of the question. He was unwilling to move west as other landed Virginians were doing. So, throughout the 1780s and 1790s, he turned ever more to the idea that somehow, through new methods and equipment, some of it of his own invention, he could improve his farming methods to keep himself from bankruptcy. "The New Husbandry," as the Enlightenment's scientific agriculture was called, was of more than academic interest to George Washington.

*B*ESIDES THE INCREASE IN POPULATION, exhausted soil was the other difficulty he faced. Washington's letter to Young is the best guide to the agricultural state of Mount Vernon in the last decade of Washington's life. "The Soil of the tract I am speaking [of], is a good loam, more inclined however to Clay than Sand," he writes. "From use, and I might add abuse, it is become more and more consolidated, and of course heavier to work. . . . A husbandman's wish would not lay the farms more level than they are, and yet some of the fields (but in no great degree) are washed into gullies, from which all of them have not, as yet, been recovered."

What stymied him was a heavy, water-resistant, slippery clay, lying under a thin layer of topsoil that, once plowed, tended to wash off the surface of the clay into the river. From reading, and from his own experiments as well as from his correspondence

MULES PLOWING A FIELD AT THE
PIONEER FARM SITE

*Breaking mules to harness and to the plow,
and plowing itself, were skilled occupations.*

FUZZY MUZZLES

*Even mules have their soft spots. Washington
was sent two stud donkeys from Europe, one
from the King of Spain, the other from the
Marquis de Lafayette.*

Corn cribs, like this one at right near the threshing barn, would hold enough ears to carry the plantation through the cold Virginia winter — and on into the next two seasons, until the corn ripened again in July. If the crop failed, Washington had to buy on the open market, a vast expense.

A CUTTING BOX

*A machine that cuts chaff into fodder for feeding cattle. From **The Complete Farmer** (London, 1769 edition).*

AN AMERICAN FARMER'S GUIDE

*J. B. Bordley, one of the preeminent exponents of the "New Husbandry," published his **Essays and Notes** in 1799. Most books on the subject were English, and their methods were subject to trial-and-error testing in American climates and soils. Bordley, who farmed in Maryland, was Washington's friend and an ideal correspondent for the master of Mount Vernon, who loved nothing better than a good jaw about agriculture and its American prospects.*

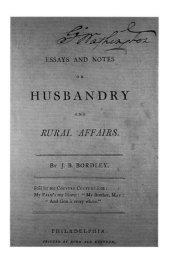

Opposite: MANURE WAGON

Spreading composted manure on the fields.

with agronomists such as Arthur Young and the American John Beale Bordley, he came to understand that the basis of sustainable farming at Mount Vernon would have to be grass — better permanent pasture that could stand up to more animals that would produce more manure to better fertilize fewer acres of cropland for a larger yield.

The soils at Mount Vernon are acid, and, since most grasses grow on alkaline, or sweet, soil, Washington saw improvement when he used alkaline fertilizers, even some as strange to contemporary ears as plaster of Paris. His aim was to augment the always scanty supply of manure, but, before the advent of pH testing, all such trials were empirical. His success rate varied widely with a range of other quite shrewd guesses, some of them garnered from his extensive agricultural reading, some from his own observations: powdered stone, herring heads and guts, mud from the river. "Green manure," meaning crops such as buckwheat, were plowed under to add humus and minerals for enrichment. In 1785 he had dreamed of finding an overseer who could "Midas like . . . convert everything he touches into manure as the first transmutation towards Gold; in a word, one who can bring worn out and gullied lands into good tilth in the shortest time."

He also came to understand that his second cultivation scheme, the three-year crop rotation (wheat, corn, and grass) he had devised, was almost as bad for the soil as his first, monocrop tobacco culture. So he went to six- and seven-year rotations, carefully computing the hours of labor and the size of the yield. He ran controlled planting experiments almost too complex to read about, much less imagine in the field. The yields never reached his expectations. In 1798, he concluded, "My Estate has been, and probably will continue to be, far from a productive one." At the same time he never ceased to harbor the hope that it could happen, if not in his lifetime.

O NE CONSTANTLY READS "Washington did," as if he did all the work himself, forgetting the people who actually "did." He was a highly self-disciplined man who demanded much of himself, and consequently he probably exacted more of his workers than many other slaveholders, though probably he was also more consistent in his treatment of them.

Changing to multicrop agriculture would have taken the Mount Vernon slaves from tobacco, with its yearly work round which Virginia slave communities had been familiar with for decades at least, into a world of new crops and livestock. Mount Vernon's black inhabitants saw no reason willingly to adopt Washington's work ethic, nor to fall enthusiastically into learning the requirements of the new crops or animal husbandry. Passivity was the only form of rebellion open to them without terrible consequences. However, learn they did, and by the end of the century many of them were no mere field hands, but rather skilled farmers, fishermen, and stockbreeders. Three of the farms had slave overseers.

THE FIGURE OF A GARDEN FORK

"This is of use for spreading and disposing the Dung . . .A Gardener can't be without it." Manure did more than fertilize the soil; a layer of it also was placed in the bottom of a hot bed, or cold frame, providing a source of heat to help young plants develop strong roots. From **The Compleat Florist,** *London, 1706.*

From a sheer enumeration of how many acres were in wheat or corn (700 each by 1788–89) or pasture (500), or from a list of crops grown, we cannot really imagine what the enormous farmscape of Mount Vernon looked like. Nor can we fully conceive of how many people worked there at once — the gangs of slave women in homespun, hoeing, grubbing, and manuring the fields, the children at harvest carrying shocks of wheat and rye, the boys herding livestock and learning to drive harrows and carts. (Over the decades, men came to have more highly differentiated jobs than women, and they worked individually on tasks more often.)

At Mount Vernon today what is called the Pioneer Farm surrounds the newly reconstructed threshing barn. It is plowed and planted just as it would have been in the eighteenth century, and, though the fields are only a few yards wide, they can give us a taste of what hand and horse cultivation looks like.

Washington's plowed fields looked rough compared to today's. With a tobacco crop, their shallow ridges and furrows were only three to four inches deep, though they looked deeper since the tobacco plants were hilled by hand for extra drainage. When he took up wheat, and later the new English methods of farming, he turned to ploughing as deep as we do today, but his fields didn't have that tabletop Midwestern look. Wide furrows separated the planted ridges by as much as four to seven feet and were intended to carry off water, meaning that much more of the land wasn't planted at all. Some farmers interplanted their wheat with corn, but Washington didn't — he'd had bad results with the practice. He did, however, interplant corn fields with rows of carrots, potatoes, turnips, or peas. Such vegetable intercropping, which retains moisture and prevents runoff, is something we are learning to do again now.

Nine plows, on average, tilled the soil at plowing time, though in peak periods the farms could mount as many as twenty-seven teams of mules, oxen, and draft horses, plus several harrows and carts, far more proportionately per acre than their neighbors. There was corn planting and haymaking in May and a second cutting of hay in mid-July. Wheat, oats, and rye were harvested in the last week of June and the first week of July. (Washington's neighbor Colonel Landon Carter, who also kept a detailed diary, thought a man could harvest four acres of wheat a day.) The harvesters worked as a team, with one man reaping, another bunching the wheat, and yet another

Opposite: THE PLANTATION BELL

"I begin my diurnal course with the Sun . . .," wrote Washington to his friend James McHenry in 1797, describing his daily routine. Every day but Sunday he expected his slaves to be at work at daybreak as well; they had a midday respite of two hours and then returned to work until nightfall.

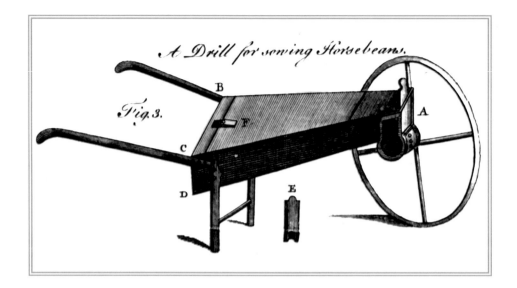

twisting straw bands around each sheaf. Extra meat was given out to all hands at harvest time as reward and celebration, and sometimes rum as well. At wheat planting time in the fall, the seed was either broadcast by hand, or "drilled," planted in rows. It took one man one day to sow an acre of wheat, Washington calculated.

*D*URING THE ALMOST FIVE DECADES that he farmed, many new tools and methods were invented to cut labor and time or to increase the yield. One of Washington's very own devices was the neat "barrel seeder," which dropped seed from a little cask as it turned the earth, making plowing and sowing a one-step operation. Washington had his plowmen mix sand in with smaller varieties to ensure thin, even coverage, just as today's gardeners do now with tiny seeds in peat cups.

On a grander scale was the enormous hay and livestock brick barn he had built at Union Farm in 1788 based on a plan sent him by Arthur Young, though, as a French visitor, Brissot de Warville, noted, "the General has much improved the plan." De Warville was impressed not only by its size, which was "one hundred feet in length and considerably more in breadth," but also by its economic construction, thanks to slave labor. ". . . it cost but three hundred pounds," said the Frenchman,

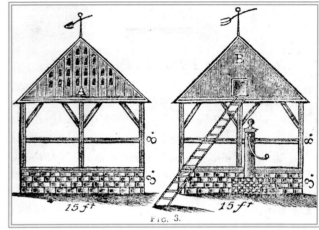

adding, "I am sure in France it would have cost three thousand." Washington, a proud man but too dignified to toot his own horn often, described his barn to Young as "equal perhaps to any in America, and for conveniences of all sorts, particularly for sheltering and feeding horses, cattle, &c., scarcely to be exceeded anywhere." His urgent reason for wanting to house livestock instead of pasturing them was to save their droppings more efficiently.

ALONG THOSE SAME LINES, recent excavations below the ha-ha between Home House and the stables have revealed a composting operation almost as glorified as its name: "stercorary." In 1787 Washington sent careful instructions to his then farm manager and nephew, George Augustine Washington, about paving the bottom of the new manure pit with cobblestones, which would prevent any composted liquids from draining away. The design of the rectangular pit, which may have been roofed with a chicken loft above (which would have added even their small droppings to the compost mix below), tallies closely with John Spurrier's advice in *The Practical Farmer*, a book that Washington owned.

A STERCORARY, OR DUNG REPOSITORY

Washington built his elegant composting device, a cobble-floored, brick-lined rectangular pit in the ground below the ha-ha near the stable. Recent archaeology has revealed postholes, indicating a roof. In 1808 Richard Peters, a friend and correspondent of Washington's, published these drawings, which show a similar structure, with a chicken roost above so the droppings could fall into the pit below. Nothing was to be wasted in the "New Husbandry." From "Remarks on the Plan of a Stercorary," by Richard Peters, Philadelphia, 1808.

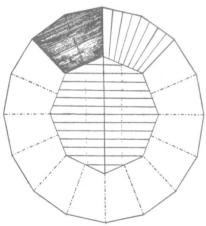

The threshing barn, built originally at Dogue Run Farm, and the mill, on the creek of the same name, are two reconstructed farm monuments that bear witness to Washington's inventiveness and his fervent desire that everything be "trim, handsome & thriving."

The step that wasted the most grain in the cycle of wheat was threshing, which for centuries had taken place on the ground and was often trod out by human feet. Washington's elegant and efficient sixteen-sided "treading house" harnessed gravity along with horses or mules. They trotted around the circular wooden floor to make the grain drop through the inch-and-a-half-wide cracks between the sturdy squared timbers into the granary below, built of 30,820 plantation-made bricks.

THE MILL, AS ELEGANT AND INNOVATIVE in its way as his Enlightenment thresher, encompasses the history of Mount Vernon as a farm, the rise of wheat as a commodity, and the cycle of use that used everything — nothing was to be thrown away if possible. This was an uncommon thing in Washington's America, where farmers' profligate practices shocked European travelers.

Washington put up with the slow old gristmill built by his father on Dogue Run until 1771 when he built a new one to manufacture flour, which he sold, in addition to wheat as a grain. He imported special French millstones, speeded the operation up by buying water rights upstream and making a new millrace, and also built a wharf to carry the expanded trade. For his plantation use and for the "country trade," his neighbors, he ground wheat and corn flour at a decent profit. For the "merchant trade," he ground fine flour to go to England and the West Indies. Always on the look-

Opposite: AGRICULTURAL ELEGANCE

The empty manure wagon pauses in front of the rebuilt treading barn and one of its attached corn cribs.

Opposite, below: THRESHING BARN PLAN

The plan for the sixteen-sided treading barn designed by George Washington and built in 1792-94.

Left: NEWFANGLED MILLWORKS

The instant that Oliver Evans patented his "Mill Machinery" in 1791, Washington invited Evans to Mount Vernon to install a set in the Dogue Run mill. From **The Young Mill-wright and Miller's Guide,** *Philadelphia, 1795.*

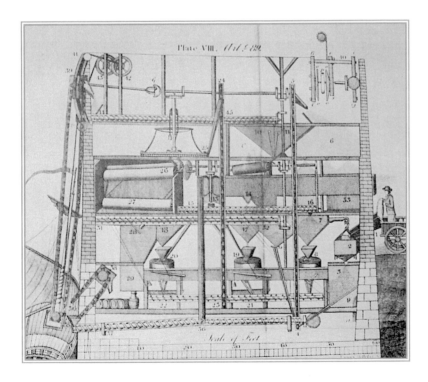

out for labor-saving devices, in 1791 he bought the very latest in patented, all-mechanical millworks, inviting its inventor, Oliver Evans, to come to Mount Vernon to install it. This was four years before Evans had even published his book on his new machinery. Besides the miller's house, the complex included a distillery (corn liquor), a cooper's shop (for barrels), hog pens, and a stable that held thirty steer. Cattle and hogs were fattened on mill refuse.

For a man like Washington, who believed in a rather distant and orderly Supreme Deity in the Enlightenment mode (though indeed he served as a vestryman for many years), farming may have offered a better private discourse of salvation than organized religion. For anyone conversant with the politics and rhetoric of the period, as Washington was, farming offered what the landscape historian Douglas D. C. Chambers calls "the rhetoric of spiritualized and regenerated landscape."

Washington had never studied Greek or Latin and would have known only in translation, if at all, Pliny the Younger's retreats, or Horace's little Sabine farm, or Virgil's "country gods, Pan and old Sylvanus, and the sisterhood of nymphs," in the Georgics. But the ideas of secular retreat and spiritual regeneration expressed in these beloved and much-quoted writings were in the air, like Freud's ideas of transference in the 1950s. Improving the land was improving the self, creating the farm was re-creating the original sacred landscape.

Like most politically attuned Americans of his day, however, he invested the idea of a sacred landscape with a larger symbolism than his own identity or personal redemption. America, in theory at least, was to be the new paradise, the place to cast off original sin as well as despotic government, the very ground to be a sacred trust for sons and daughters.

But for Washington it was different. He had no direct heirs, and, by the terms of his will, he even divided the lands he had amassed so diligently. Isn't it reasonable to suppose that he thought his legacy would not be his farm, but farming itself? Ninety percent of the American population were farmers in 1790, so the way to a strong America clearly seemed to be through better husbandry. He wanted his farming to be a model not just for his neighbors, but for his country, so it could become the "storehouse and granary of the world."

Opposite: Virginia red cedars at sunset

The rural idyll, when work is done at the end of day.

Passiflora caerulea

On the way home from his daily plantation round, Washington would have seen the exotic-looking flowers of the May-pop, the passionflower vine **(Passiflora incarnata)** *at the edges of the woods. It is a hardy cousin of this tropical, sky blue version, which was grown in conservatories. From* **Curtis' Botanical Magazine,** *Vol. 1, London, 1793.*

Washington knew that everything he did set a precedent. What he wrote in 1789 about his presidential duties could be applied just as well to how he farmed: "I walk on untrodden ground. There is scarcely any part of my conduct which may not hereafter be drawn into precedent." Agricultural reform, which he thought would eventually right the soil at Mount Vernon, heralded the idea that other wrongs could eventually be righted also: slavery could be abolished, for example, not just by personal fiat as he freed his own slaves by the terms of his will, but by law.

PEERING BACKWARDS into the creation of Mount Vernon's landscape, gardens, and farms as if together they really did form a portrait of the man, we discern the same process of growth everywhere. His philosophy of life deepened, and we note the severe though ceremonial plantation framework of his hard-driving early years giving way to a larger, more tender concept of landscape for ornament and delight, as well as use. His politics changed radically, and here we can agree with one of his biographers, James Flexner, who writes that by the 1760s we are looking at a man who had called England "home" coming to the conclusion that Americans were no longer British, an idea reflected in Washington's determined efforts to break free economically from a system that made him a second-class citizen. Moving on from that thought, we can note, as many historians have done, Washington's inability to separate theory from practice — he was never a theoretician, and we've seen that the minute he read about a way to graft or plant or plow that seemed good to him, he tried to do it. In fact, the actuality of making was the business of his life. It is not a stretch to say that making a landscape requires many of the same qualities as making war, or a nation. Last of all, we might notice that Washington, like every good gardener and every wise statesman, understood that creation wasn't a perfect process. He didn't especially like the Constitution that came out of the Constitutional Congress, but he thought it was workable, and maybe even improvable down the road, much like the bowling green he seeded just before it rained, when some of the seed floated away. He re-seeded — and it rained again — and so on and so forth, until it was green at last.

THE FARMER

Washington's iconization as "Father of his Country," and as what might be called the First Farmer took place during his lifetime. After his death, there was an outpouring of popular prints such as this that further enshrined every detail of his life. Detail of **George Washington the Farmer,** *from a series of lithographs,* **The Life of George Washington,** *by Claude Regnier after Junius Brutus Stearns, 1853.*

A EWE AND HER LAMB IN MAY

*M*AKING PLANS FOR HIS FARMS AND LANDSCAPE GARDEN was among the last things Washington did in December 1799, the year of his death. Some of the final entries in his papers were the projected details of field usage and crop rotations for 1800–1803. Deciding which trees to cut and which to save down by the river below the house, where he intended to put an ornamental fishpond and a new gravel walk, was what kept him out in a wet snowfall on that Friday, December 13. The following day he died at home of an acute throat infection, with Martha at the foot of the bed, and Tobias Lear holding his hand.

But to leave him at his lively best in his "innocent and useful pursuits" we can turn to a letter of March 1781, filled with the hectic pleasures of the imagination

Opposite: MOUNT VERNON FROM
THE POTOMAC RIVER

*Today in early December, the Canada geese rest
on the waters, having flown south here for the
winter. Washington had the same homing instincts
for Mount Vernon: in his imagination, this picture
must have often floated before him, along with its
promises of sustenance, beauty, work, and pleasure.*

Right: AN ESPALIERED CHERRY TREE
IN THE UPPER GARDEN

*"Cherries, Plumbs, Pears and Apples bloomed
forth," an observation Washington happily made,
spring after spring, in his journal.*

that every gardener knows in spring. When he wrote it, he was far away from his "Vine & Fig tree," during a period of the war bracketed by the mutiny of his own dispirited troops in January and punishing raids carried out in Virginia in April by the traitor Benedict Arnold.

"How many Lambs have you had this Spring? How many colts are you like to have?" he wrote to Lund Washington. "Is your covered ways done? What are you going about next? Have you any prospect of getting paint and Oyl? Are you going to repair the Pavement of the Piazza? Is anything doing, or like to be done with respect to the Wall at the edge of the Hill in front of the house? Have you made good the decayed Trees at the ends of the House, in the Hedges &ca. Have you made any attempts to reclaim more land for the meadow? &ca. &ca. An acct. of these things would be satisfactory to me, and infinitely amusing in the recital, as I have these kind of improvements very much at heart."

George Washington's Trees and Shrubs

During his forty-five years at Mount Vernon, Washington was an inveterate tree planter. The eighteenth century was a period of such experimentation as we can't imagine in our own gardens: instead of handy zone maps and garden-center perennnials marked with cultural directions, there was a joyful sense that anything that could be tried, should be tried. A few of the 108 species listed here, such as the live oak *(Quercus virginiana)* were native to more southern zones; Washington sought them out eagerly, writing to friends and relations for seeds, cuttings, and

LIRIODENDRON TULIPIFERA

even young specimens. Needless to say, they did not succeed. Others, such as the weeping willow *(Salix babylonica,* newly introduced and highly fashionable in Washington's day), were species he had seen on his travels or heard about from fellow landscape-garden enthusiasts. But by far the largest number of the trees and shrubs on this list are American regional natives remarked on by Washington on his daily rides and transplanted by the Mount Vernon slaves.

Acer pensylvanicum	Striped maple	T
A. rubrum	Swamp maple	T
A. saccharum	Sugar maple	T
Aesculus hippocastanum	Horse chestnut	T
A. × hybrida	Redflowered buckeye	T
A. flava	Yellow buckeye	T
A. parviflora	Bottlebrush buckeye	S
Amelanchier canadensis	Thicket serviceberry	T
A. arborea	Downy serviceberry	S
Aronia arbutifolia	Red chokeberry	S
Asimina triloba	Pawpaw	T
Buxus sempervirens	Boxwood	S
B. sempervirens 'Pendula'	Weeping boxwood	S
B. sempervirens 'Suffruticosa'	Dwarf edging boxwood	S
Calycanthus floridus	Carolina allspice, sweet shrub	S
Carya illinoensis	Pecan	T
C. laciniosa	Shellbark hickory	T
C. ovata	Shagbark hickory	T
Catalpa bignoniodes	Southern catalpa	T
Cercis canadensis	Eastern redbud	T

CERCIS CANADENSIS

Chimonanthus praecox	Fragrant wintersweet	S
Chionanthus virginicus	Fringe tree	T
Cornus alba	Tatarian dogwood	S
C. florida	Flowering dogwood	T
C. mas	Cornelian cherry	T
Cotinus coggygria	Smoke tree	S
Crataegus laevigata	English hawthorn	T
C. phaenopyrum	Washington hawthorn	T
C. punctata	Thicket hawthorn	T
Cytisus scoparius	Scotch broom	S
Euonymus atropurpureus	Burning bush	S
Exochorda racemosa	Pearlbush	S
Franklinia alatamaha	Franklinia	T
Fraxinus americana	White ash	T
Gleditsia triancanthos var. *inermis*	Honey locust	T
Gymnocladus dioicus	Kentucky coffeetree	T
Halesia carolina	Carolina silver-bell	T
Hibiscus syriacus	Rose-of-Sharon	S
Hydrangea arborescens	Wild hydrangea	S
H. quercifolia	Oak-leaf hydrangea	S
Ilex aquifolium	English holly	T
I. opaca	American holly	T
I. verticillata	Winterberry	S
I. vomitoria	Yaupon holly	S
Itea virginica	Virginia sweetspire	S
Juglans nigra	Black walnut	T
Juniperus virginiana	Eastern red cedar	T

KALMIA LATIFOLIA

Kalmia latifolia   Mountain laurel   S
Kerria japonica 'Pleniflora'   Japanese kerria   S

Lagerstroemia indica   Crapemyrtle   T
Laurus nobilis   Bay laurel   T
Leucothoe axillaris   Coast leucothoe   S
Lindera benzoin   Spicebush   S
Liriodendron tulipifera   Tulip poplar   T
Lonicera sempervirens   Scarlet honeysuckle   Vine

Magnolia grandiflora   Southern magnolia   T
Malus coronaria   Wild sweet crabapple   T
Melia azedarach   Chinaberry   T
Morus alba   White mulberry   T
Myrica pensylvanica   Northern bayberry   S

Nyssa sylvatica   Black tupelo   T

Ostrya virginiana   American hop hornbeam   T

Philadelphus coronarius   Sweet mock orange   S
Pinus strobus   White pine   T
P. virginiana   Virginia pine   T
Platycladus orientalis   Oriental arborvitae   S
Populus nigra 'Italica'   Lombardy poplar   T
Prunus angustifolia   Chickasaw plum
P. cerasifera   Cherry plum   T
P. insititia   Damson plum   T
P. maritima   Beach plum   S
P. serotina   Black cherry   T
Ptelea trifoliata   Water-ash   T
Punica granatum   Pomegranate   T
Pyracantha coccinea   Scarlet firethorn   S

Quercus nigra   Water oak   T
Q. prinus   Chestnut oak   T
Q. velutina   Black oak   T
Q. virginiana   Live oak   T

Rhododendron periclymenoides   Pinxterbloom   T
Robinia pseudoacacia   Locust, Black locust   T
Rosa eglanteria   Sweetbriar   S

MORUS ALBA

SYRINGA VULGARIS

Salix alba 'Vitellina'   Yellow willow   T
S. babylonica   Weeping willow   T
Sassafras albidum   Sassafras   T
Symphoricarpos orbiculatus   Indiancurrant coralberry   S
Syringa × persica   Persian lilac   S
S. vulgaris   Common lilac   S

Taxodium distichum   Common bald cypress   T
Taxus baccata   English yew   T
Thuja occidentalis   American arborvitae   T
Tilia americana   American linden   T
T. cordata   Littleleaf linden   T
Tsuga canadensis   Canadian hemlock   T

Ulmus americana   American elm   T
U. serotina   Red elm   T

Viburnum lentago   Sheepberry   S
V. opulus   Guelder rose   S
V. prunifolium   Blackhaw viburnum   S

Eighteenth-Century Flowers

ALL PLANTS AND BULBS LISTED HERE were used in American gardens in Washington's time. Asterisks indicate a mention in his writings or correspondence. How few, to today's eyes, are the numbers of flowers mentioned by comparison with his extensive lists of trees and shrubs!

Many have wondered why, and whether the division was by preference, as in "he just didn't care about flowers, " or by gender: his/hers, George's /Martha's, landscape/flowers. That's too simple. The threads are tangled: custom, class, and individual preference must have all played their part.

Women had charge of the household, which included the garden, an enclosed space filled with more vegetables than flowers, at least up until the middle of the eighteenth century. There were women, such as Lady Jean Skipwith of Prestwold, Virginia, who were vitally interested in flowers, but Martha's scanty remaining correspondence mentions the garden only as a place where ingredients for medicine and cookery were grown. However, whatever her conception of the garden was, we can imagine that she had considerable oversight there when she was at home, perhaps communicating with the gardener herself. (The weekly accounts of tasks and expenses were nonetheless submitted to her husband.) His correspondence also mentions seeds and plants passed along or requested for her, and there is one tantalizing account-book reference about her "visiting gardens."

In the tiny world of upper-class American gardening in the late eighteenth century, if there was what could grandly be termed an aesthetic hierarchy, the landscape garden certainly topped the list. For the governing elite, a "prospect," one of those extensive views of hill and vale framed by trees à la Claude Lorraine, easily outshone a view of a useful garden crowded with roses and peas, no matter how pretty. And Washington was interested in display, the kind of display that showed him off as a man of substance.

As we have seen, however, he was also a man who deeply loved trees and shrubs. Even his rather stolid diary style occasionally loosens up when he describes his favorites, both in his orchards and in the wild: ". . . all nature seemed alive," he wrote on April 25, 1785. "Cherries, Plumbs, Pears & Apples bloomed forth and the forest trees in general were displaying their foliage." There are no similar effusions about flowers from George's own pen. What we know about Mount Vernon's flowery gardens comes mostly from visitors' accounts, especially later ones.

Plant List

Achillea millifolium	Yarrow
A. ptarmica	Sneezewort
Adonis aestivalis	Pheasant's eye
Ageratum houstonianum	Ageratum
Alcea rosea	Hollyhock
Amaranthus caudatus	Love-lies-bleeding
A. tricolor	Joseph's coat
Antirrhinum majus	Snapdragon
Aquilegia canadensis	Wild columbine
Arabis alpina	Rock cress
Armeria maritima	Thrift
Aster nova-angliae	New England aster
Aurinia saxatilis	Basket-of-gold
Baptisia australis	Blue false indigo
Belamcanda chinensis	Blackberry lily
Browallia speciosa	Bush violet
Calendula officinalis	Pot marigold
Callistephus chinensis	China aster
Campanula persicifolia	Peach-leaved bellflower
Catharanthus roseus	Rose periwinkle
Celosia cristata	Crested cockscomb
C. plumosa	Spiked cockscomb
Centaurea cyanus	Cornflower
C. moschata var. suaveolens	Sweet sultan
Cerastium tomentosum	Snow-in-summer
Cheiranthus cheiri	Wallflower
Chrysanthemum frutescens	Marguerite
Cleome hassleriana	Spider flower
Consolida ambigua	Rocket larkspur
Coreopsis verticillata	Tickseed
★ *Delphinium ajacis*	Larkspur
Dianthus barbatus	Sweet William
D. caryophyllus	Clove pink
D. chinensis	Rainbow pink
D. plumarius	Cottage pink
★ *Digitalis purpurea*	Common foxglove
Dolichos lablab	Hyacinth bean

ECHINACEA PURPUREA

Echinacea purpurea	Purple coneflower
Echinops ritro	Globe thistle
Eryngium maritimum	Sea holly
Gaillardia artistata	Blanket flower
Gomphrena globosa	Globe amaranth
Heliotropum arborescens	Heliotrope
Hemerocallis fulva	Orange daylily
Hesperis matronalis	Sweet rocket
Hibiscus coccineus	Hibiscus
Iberis sempervirens	Candytuft
Impatiens balsamina	Balsam
Iris germanica	German iris
I. siberica	Siberian iris
I. versicolor	Blue flag
Lantana camara	Prickly lantana
★ *Lathyrus latifolius*	Everlasting pea

Lavatera trimestris	Spanish blush mallow
Lavendula angustifolia	English lavender
Lilium candidum	Madonna lily
Linum perenne	Blue perennial flax
★ *Lobelia cardinalis*	Cardinal flower
Lobularia maritima	Sweet alyssum
Lunaria annua	Honesty
Lychnis chalcedonica	Maltese cross
L. coronaria	Rose campion
L. flos-cuculi	Ragged robin
Mattiola incana	Common stock
Mertensia virginica	Virginia bluebell
Mirabilis jalapa	Four o'clock
Monarda fistulosa	Wild bergamot
Nepeta mussini	Catmint
Nigella damascena	Love-in-a-mist
Paeonia officinalis	Peony
Papaver orientale	Oriental poppy
P. rhoeas	Flanders poppy
★ *Phlox divaricata*	Wild sweet William
★ *P. paniculata*	Perennial phlox
Platycodon grandiflorus	Balloon flower
Primula × polyantha	Polyanthus primrose
Primula vulgaris	English primrose
Ranunculus asiaticus	Persian buttercup
Rudbeckia hirta	Black-eyed Susan
Salvia officinalis	Sage
S. sclarea	Clary sage
Scabiosa atropurpurea	Pincushion flower
Stachys byzantina	Lamb's ears

Stokesia laevis	Stokes' aster
Tagetes erecta	African marigold
T. patula	French marigold
Tanacetum vulgare	Tansy
Thalictrum aquilegifolium	Meadow rue
T. flavum	Yellow meadow rue
Tropaeolum majus	Garden nasturtium
Valeriana officinalis	Garden heliotrope
Vinca rosea	Madagascar periwinkle
Viola odorata	Sweet violet
V. tricolor	Johnny-jump-up
Xeranthemum annuum	Common immortelle
★ *Yucca filamentosa*	Adam's needle
Zinnia angustifolia	Angustifolia zinnia
Z. multiflora	Many-flowered zinnia
Z. peruviana	Peruvian zinnia

HEMEROCALLIS FLAVA

Bulbs Grown Today at Mount Vernon

Amaryllis belladonna	Belladonna lily, Naked lady	*Muscari argaei* 'Album'	White grape hyacinth
Anemone coronaria	Windflower	*M. armeriacum*	Grape hyacinth
Convallaria majalis	Lily-of-the-valley	*Narcissus cyclamineus* 'February Gold'	'February Gold' jonquil
Crocus tommasinianus	Species crocus	*N. × odorus*	Campernelle jonquil
C. vernus	Dutch crocus	*N. × odorus* 'Plenus'	Double campernelle jonquil
Eranthis hyemalis	Winter aconite	*Narcissus* ssp.	**Jonquils:** 'Unsurpassable', 'Actaea'
★ *Fritillaria imperialis*	Crown imperial	*Ornithogalum nutans*	Silverbell
Galanthus nivalis	Snowdrop	*O. umbellatum*	Star of Bethlehem
Hyacinthoides hispanica	Spanish bluebells	*Polianthes tuberosa*	Tuberose
Hyacinthus orientalis	Common hyacinth	*Scilla bifolia* 'Rosea'	Squill, pink form
Iris latifolia	English iris	*S. siberica*	Siberian squill
I. pallida	Dalmatian iris	★ *Tulipa gesneriana*	Species tulip
I. pumila	Dwarf bearded iris	*Tulipa* ssp.	**Tulips:** 'Allegretto', 'Flaming Parrot',
I. xiphium	Dutch iris		'Generaal de Wet', 'Georgette'
Lilium candidum	Madonna lily		'Keizerskroon', Rembrandt-type

FRITILLARIA IMPERIALIS

Old Roses Grown Today at Mount Vernon

Rosa alba	White rose of York	*R. × francofurtana*	'Empress Josephine' rose
R. centifolia muscosa	Moss rose	*R. gallica* 'Pompon de Bourgogne'	Burgundian rose
R. chinensis 'Old Blush'	'Old Blush' rose	*R. gallica* 'Tuscany'	Old Velvet rose
R. damascena 'Celsiana'	'Celsiana' rose	*R. gallica* 'Versicolor'	Rosa mundi
R. eglanteria	Sweetbriar	*R. pimpinellifolia*	Scotch Briar

Right: ROSA GALLICA 'VERSICOLOR'

Botanical Garden Plant List

THIS LIST, compiled from George Washington's own notes on what he grew from seed, gives an idea of his breadth of interest in plants, mostly trees and crops. The common names are those he used.

Acacia cavenia or *A. farnesiana*	Acacia
Avena fatua	Wild oats
Beta vulgaris var. *macrorhiza*	Mangel-wurzel
Calycanthus floridus	Carolina allspice
Capsicum annuum (Longum group)	Cayenne pepper
C. annuum var. *glabriusculum* (Longum group)	Bird pepper
Caesalpina pulcherrima	Flower fence
Carya illinoiensis	Illinois nut/pecan
C. ovata	Shagbark hickory
Cassia chamaecrista	Partridge peas
Chichorium intybus	Chicorium
Hura crepitans	Sandbox tree
Jatropha curcas	Physic nut/Barbados nut
Juniperus virginiana	Red cedar
Lathyrus grandiflorus:	Everlasting peas
L. latifolius	
L. sylvestris	
L. odoratus	Painted lady pea
Ligustrum vulgare	Common privet
Magnolia acuminata	Cucumber magnolia
M. grandiflora	Southern magnolia
Medicago sativa	Lucerne
Melia azederach	Pride of China
Onobrychis vicifolia	Sainfoin
Panicum maximum	Guinea corn or Grass
Pinus virginiana	Virginia pine
Pistacia vera	Pistachio
Poa trivialis	Birding grass
Populus nigra 'Italica'	Lombardy poplar
Quercus nigra	Water oak
Q. virginiana	Live oak
Rheum rhaponticum	Rhubarb
Sabal palmetto or *S. umbraculifera*	Palmetto
Trifolium stoloniferum	Kentucky clover
Ulex europaeus or *U. gallii*	Furze

SEEDS OF *RUDBECKIA HIRTA*

The Vegetables, Herbs, and Fruits Grown at Mount Vernon

Vegetables and Herbs

Anise
Artichokes, French
Asparagus
Balm, lemon
Basil, sanctum
Basil, sweet
Beans, bush
Beans, bush lima
Beans, pole lima
Beets
Broccoli
Cabbage
Caraway
Carrots
Catnip
Cauliflower
Chives
Cucumbers
Germander
Horseradish
Hyssop
Kale
Lavender
Lavender cotton
Lettuce, loose leaf
Lovage
Marjoram
Nasturtiums
Okra

CABBAGE

Onions
Oregano
Parsley
Parsnips
Peas
Pennyroyal
Peppers, cayenne
Peppers, sweet
 or bird
Potatoes, Irish
Potatoes, sweet
Radish
Rhubarb
Rosemary
Rue
Rutabaga
Sage
Salsify
Spinach
Squash, summer
Swiss chard
Tarragon
Thyme, common
Thyme, French
Thyme, golden
Thyme, silver
Tomatoes
Turnips
Winter Savory

THE LOWER GARDEN

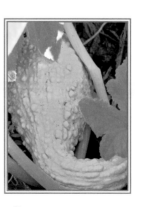

CROOKNECK SQUASH

Fruits

Apples
Apricots
Cherries
Currants
Figs
Grapes
Nectarines
Peaches
Pears
Plums
Quince
Raspberries
Strawberries

SCARLET STRAWBERRY

Espalier fruits

Wall trees:
 Apples
 Apricots
 Cherries
 Nectarines
 Peaches
 Pears
Cordons:
 Apples
 Pears

ROYAL GEORGE PEACH

1674 John Washington, George's great-grand-father, is granted the Mount Vernon homesite.

1726 Augustine Washington, George's father, acquires the property from his sister Mildred.

1732 George, first child of Augustine and Mary Ball Washington, born at the family place on the Potomac River in Westmoreland County, Virginia.

1735–39 Augustine in residence at Mount Vernon with his young family.

1743 Augustine dies; Lawrence Washington, George's elder half-brother, marries and settles at Mount Vernon.

1744 Joseph Addison's essays from *The Spectator* on "the Pleasures of the Imagination" and the "beautiful Wildness of Nature" (London, 1711–12) published as a set, which George later owned.

1749 Martha Dandridge, b. 1731, marries Daniel Parke Custis, son of John Custis of Williamsburg, whose four-acre pleasure garden was one of the best in the colonies. John Custis died in 1749, but Martha must have known this garden during her seven-year Custis marriage.

1752 Lawrence dies at Mount Vernon.

1754 Leases Mount Vernon from Lawrence's widow, the sister of George William Fairfax, at nearby Belvoir.

1753–58 Periodically absent from Mount Vernon in the French and Indian War.

1758 Resigns from the Virginia Regiment. Elected for the first time to the Virginia House of Burgesses.

1759 Marries Martha Dandridge Custis. With her two children, settles at Mount Vernon.

1759 Buys Batty Langley's *New Principles of Gardening*. Later adds Philip Miller's *Abridgement of the Gardener's Dictionary* (1771), and Thomas Mawe & John Abercrombie's *The Universal Gardener and Botanist* (1778).

1761 Inherits Mount Vernon following the death of Lawrence's widow.

1761 Lower rectangular garden in existence.

1762 Lower garden walled.

1763 Upper rectangular garden in existence but not completely enclosed.

1765–75 Almost continuously a member of the Virginia House of Burgesses in Williamsburg; a good opportunity to see the pleasure gardens and houses of the capital. Resides at former John Custis house when in attendance.

1766 Abandons tobacco as staple crop; succeeds with mixed farming.

1775 Elected general to command all Continental forces. Lund Washington, George's cousin, manages plantation during war years and continues with second building and landscape program initiated in 1774.

1770s Creates vineyard.

1776 Upper garden walled completely.

1776 Orders planting of north and south groves.

1781 Stops briefly at Mount Vernon en route to and from Yorktown.

1783 Resigns his commission to Congress and retires to Mount Vernon.

1783–89 Personally supervises transformation of his new landscape garden. Raises house to three stories; swings back outbuildings into present north and south lanes.

1785	First mention of "my little garden," the botanical garden.
1785–6	Remodels driveway in serpentine form. Rectangular garden walls rebuilt as curves. "Wildernesses" planted.
1785	Measures the deer park or paddock; builds serpentine wall.
1780s	Constructs ha-ha walls and ditches.
Mid-1780s	Beds and fruit garden planted in "Vineyard Inclosure."

1784–5	Constructs conservatory.
1787	Presides over the Constitutional Convention in Philadelphia.
1789–97	Years of the presidency. Visits Mount Vernon fifteen times.
1799	Dies and is buried in the old family vault at Mount Vernon.
1800	Ahead of schedule, Martha begins to free the slaves mentioned in George's will as his. (By the terms of his will, they were to be set free at her death.)

1802	Martha dies and is buried beside him. Mount Vernon passes to Bushrod Washington, a nephew.
1829	Bushrod Washington dies, leaving Mount Vernon to his nephew John Augustine Washington.
1853	Mount Vernon Ladies' Association founded.
1858	Mount Vernon Ladies' Association receives its final charter from the Commonwealth of Virginia and purchases Mount Vernon.

WASHINGTONS'S SKETCH FOR THE
DEER PARK WALL

His long absences have left us a stream of letters, directives, and sketches that document how he shaped the landscape. This sketch included instructions on how to lay out a serpentine wall to keep his herd of deer safely within their enclosure below the house on the side facing the river.

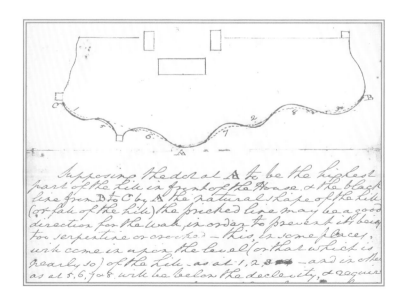

Chapter One

PAGE 9

"No Virginian can talk on any subject," William Maclay, *The Diary of William Maclay and Other Notes on Senate Debates,* ed. Kenneth R. Bowling and Helen E. Veit, (Baltimore: Johns Hopkins University Press, 1988), vol. IX: 258.

PAGE 10

Anyone who thinks things through: For a discussion of hero types and the present-day preference for heroes with flaws, see Garry Wills, *Cincinnatus: George Washington and the Enlightenment* (Garden City, N.Y.: Doubleday & Co., 1984), 109-32.

That's very unlike Washington's carefully shaped decorum: For a discussion of Washington's manners and morals and the influence of his schoolboy copywork on him, see Richard Brookhiser, *Founding Father: Rediscovering George Washington* (New York: The Free Press, 1996), 121-36.

"He seems to come from another time," Gordon S. Wood, "The Greatness of George Washington" *The Virginia Quarterly Review* 68, no. 2 (Spring 1992), 190-91.

PAGE 11

"None . . . were to be seen," George Washington (hereafter GW), 6 April 1786, *The Diaries of George Washington* (hereafter *Diaries*), ed. Donald Jackson and Dorothy Twohig (Charlottesville: University Press of Virginia, 1976–79), vol. III: 37–38.

PAGE 13

"to disperse the families I have an aversion," GW to Robert Lewis, August 18, 1799, *The Writings of George Washington* (hereafter *Writings*), ed. John C. Fitzpatrick (Washington, D.C.: United States Government Printing Office, 1931-40), vol. 37: 338-39.

modern Cincinnatus: Wills, *Cincinnatus*, 12-16, 36-7. From the moment GW resigned his military commission on December 23, 1783 to return to Mount Vernon and private life, he was often presented in word and image as that personification of virtue, Cincinnatus. According to legend, the fifth-century-B.C. Roman patriot twice left his plow to command troops to protect Rome successfully, each time returning to his small farm afterward.

PAGE 14

Berkeley, Shirley and Westover: These typical massive and beautifully detailed brick Georgian plantation complexes of the first half of the eighteenth century were built along the James River by the most powerful Virginia dynasties, such as the Carters and were testimony to a successful economy based on tobacco and slaves. All three houses exist today.

"She well deserved to be the companion," Peter Stephen Du Ponceau, September 9, 1837, recollection of a Mount Vernon visit in 1780, "The Autobiography of Peter Stephen Du Ponceau," *Pennsylvania Magazine of History and Biography* 63 (July 1939), 313.

"She is small and fat," Claude Blanchard, *The Journal of Claude Blanchard, Commissary of the French Auxiliary Army sent to the United States during the American Revolution, 1780–1783,* trans. William Duane, ed. Thomas Balch (Albany, N.Y.: 1876), 66.

"she is plain in her dress," Abigail Adams to her sister, July 12, 1789, *New Letters of Abigail Adams, 1788–1801,* ed. Stewart Mitchell (Boston: Houghton Mifflin Co., 1947), 13.

PAGE 19

"planted without any order or regularity," GW to Lund Washington, August 19, 1776, *Writings*, vol. 5: 460-1.

"of all the clever trees (especially flowering ones) that can be got," ibid.

PAGE 20

"Virginia ladies value themselves on the goodness of their bacon," GW to Marquis de Lafayette, June 8, 1786, *Writings,* vol. 28: 457.

PAGE 29

"every thing in his garden that will be nessary . . ." MW to Fanny Bassett Washington, July 1, 1792, "Worthy Partner," *The Papers of Martha Washington,* comp. Joseph E. Fields (Westport, Conn.: Greenwood Press, 1994), 239.

PAGE 30

"The Gift Outright," Robert Frost, from *The Witness Tree,* in *Robert Frost: Collected Poems, Prose, & Plays,* comp. Richard Poirier and Mark Richardson (New York: The Library of America, 1995), 316.

Chapter Two

PAGE 32

"The whole plantation, the garden, and the rest," Julian Ursyn Niemcewicz, *Under Their Vine and Fig Tree: Travels through America in 1797–1799, 1805 with some further account of life in New Jersey,* ed. and trans. Metchie J. E. Budka (Elizabeth, N.J.: Grassman Publishing Co., 1965), vol. 14: 65. Niemcewicz was aide-de-camp to the Polish hero Tadeusz Kosciuszko during the Polish uprising of 1794; he visited Mount Vernon for twelve days in 1798.

PAGE 36

"the aimiable Simplicity of unadorned nature," Alexander Pope, "Essay from The Guardian (1713)," in *The Genius of the Place: The English Landscape Garden, 1620–1820,* ed. John Dixon Hunt and Peter Willis (New York: Harper & Row, 1975), 205.

PAGE 37

"I am now I believe fixd at this seat with an agreeable Consort for Life," GW to Richard Washington, September 20, 1759, *Writings,* vol. 2: 337.

PAGE 40

"none of the important events," GW to Sarah Cary Fairfax, May 16, 1798, *Writings,* vol. 36: 263.

PAGE 42

"to find more happiness in retirement than I ever experienc'd," GW to Richard Washington, September 20, 1759, *Writings,* vol. 2: 337.

Garry Wills, the historian, has pointed out: Wills, *Cincinnatus,* 3-16, 87-89.

PAGE 44

"power was acceptable," Robert F. Dalzell Jr., "Constructing Independence: Monticello, Mount Vernon, and the Men Who Built Them," *Eighteenth-Century Studies* 26, no.4 (Summer 1993), 572.

"very thick woods remain standing," Isaac Weld, *Travels through the States of North America and the Provinces of Upper and Lower Canada, during the years 1795, 1796, and 1797* (London: John Stockdale, 1799), vol. 1: 90-1.

PAGE 48

"The indispensable man," James Thomas Flexner, *Washington: The Indispensable Man* (Boston: Little, Brown and Company, 1969, reprint, Boston: First Back Bay Edition, 1974).

"reserve and coldness . . . drew me towards him by every tender and endearing tie," 4 March 1788, Tobias Lear to William Prescott, in *Mount Vernon Ladies' Association of the Union Annual Report 1958,* 22.

PAGE 51

"At two o'clock the General arrived on the back of a gray horse." *Under Their Vine and Fig Tree,* 96.

PAGE 53

". . . when we came down the Hill to the Plantation of Mr. Thos Gist," October 13, 1770 *Diaries,* vol. I: 288.

PAGE 55

"After dinner we soon began to mount up," John Bartram, *John and William Bartram's America: Selections from the Writings of the Philadelphia Naturalists,* ed. Helen Gere Cruickshank (New York: Devin-Adair Company, 1957), 40.

PAGE 57

"On approaching these shades," William Bartram, "Travels through North and South Carolina, Georgia, East and West Florida, etc.," in *William Bartram: Travels and Other Writings,* ed. Thomas P. Slaughter (New York: The Library of America, 1996), 280.

". . . the most barren country I ever beheld. . . ." April 24, 1791, *Diaries,* vol. VI: 118-119.

Chapter Three

PAGE 63

"The blossom of the Red bud are just beginning to display," April 26, 1785, *Diaries,* vol. IV: 128.

PAGE 66

"I will receive with pleasure and gratitude the seeds of any trees and shrubs," GW to George William Fairfax, June 26, 1786, *Writings,* vol. 28: 469.

PAGE 67

". . . twelve horse chestnuts, twelve box cuttings,"

Col. Henry Lee Jr. to GW, March 12, 1785, *The Papers of George Washington* (hereafter *Papers*), ed. W. W. Abbot and Dorothy Twohig, Confederation Series (Charlottesville: University Press of Virginia, 1992), vol. 2: 431.

"stored with many curious plants, shrubs and trees," June 10, 1787, *Diaries,* vol. V: 166.

"did not answer my expectations," October 10, 1789, *Diaries,* vol. V: 458.

PAGE 68

"thick enough for the limbs to interlock when the Trees are grown," GW to Lund Washington, December 17, 1776, *Writings,* vol. 37: 537.

PAGE 70

"rows of trees exactly corrisponding with each other," Amariah Frost, "A Day At Mount Vernon, in 1797," ed. Hamilton B. Staples (Worcester, Mass., 1879), 11.

"Road to my Mill Swamp," January 12, 1785, *Diaries,* vol. IV: 75.

PAGE 73

"exceedingly miry and bad working," February 8, 1785, *Diaries,* vol. IV: 86.

"they have been more accustomed to bear drought," GW to Lund Washington, December 25, 1782, *Writings,* vol. 25: 472–3.

PAGE 74

"A Journal of my Journey over the Mountains

began Fryday," March 11, 1747, *Diaries,* vol. I: 6.

"The plan describes with accuracy the houses, walks," GW to Samuel Vaughan, November 12, 1787, *Writings,* vol. 29: 313.

PAGE 75

Dancing school: Brookhiser, *Founding Father,* 111. See Brookhiser's section entitled "Nature" for Washington's physical attributes and how they defined his presence and his character.

PAGE 76

Melancholy: for a description of Washington as "impressive, majestic, with a mildness that indicated moral qualities and a shade of sadness that gave him an interesting air," see Flexner, *Washington,* 140.

"Washington's defense against melancholy remained movement," Flexner, *Washington,* 183–4.

"Those trees which my hands have planted," GW to the Chevalier de Chastellux, June 2, 1784, *Writings,* vol. 27: 413.

PAGE 79

"His success . . . was the triumph of a man," Flexner, *Washington,* 180.

Chapter Four

PAGE 81

"a neat flower garden laid out in squares," Benjamin Henry Latrobe, *The Virginia Journals of Benjamin Henry Latrobe, 1795–1798,* ed. Edward C. Carter

II, (New Haven: Yale University Press, 1977), vol. 1: 165.

PAGE 84

"no other guide but his eye to direct his choice," GW to William Thornton, December 30, 1798, *Writings,* vol. 37: 79.

PAGE 85

"having assembled the men from my plantations," February 4, 1786, *Diaries,* vol. IV: 271.

PAGE 87

"Brockley, collyflower, leaks," Samuel Vaughan, November 12, 1787, "The Journal of Samuel Vaughan," from a facsimile in the Library of Congress.

PAGE 91

"Kitchen and Flower gardens abounding," Winthrop Sargent, October 13, 1793, private diary of Winthrop Sargent, transcript courtesy the Mount Vernon Ladies' Association.

PAGE 94

many polite, almost anguished letters: The correspondence with "Mrs. Margaret Carroll" of Mount Clare began on September 16, 1789, with a letter from Washington tentatively accepting her offer of plants from her conservatory. It continues through many exchanges in which Washington protests that she is giving him too many plants and thereby robbing herself, and Mrs. Carroll protests that filling his greenhouse is such an honor that she can't resist adding this or that. It concludes on November 22, 1789, when Washington writes to Otho Holland Williams, Mrs. Carroll's agent, telling him that he "can not refuse the kind and pressing offer of bearing fruit Trees from the good Lady . . ."

PAGE 95

"five boxes, and twenty small pots of trees," Otho H. Williams to GW, October 29, 1789, *Papers,* Presidential Series, vol. 4: 40

PAGE 97

"Planted and sowed in boxes," April 13, 1785, *Diaries,* vol. IV: 118.

PAGE 98

"taken from the nearest Pit," GW to Anthony Whiting, October 14, 1792, *Writings,* vol. 32: 178.

Chapter Five

PAGE 103

"I saw there for the first time preserved strawberries," Peter Stephen Du Ponceau, "Autobiography," 313.

PAGE 104

"I do not desire any of your fine fellows," GW to Robert Cary and Company, November 22, 1771, *Writings,* vol. 3: 75.

PAGE 105

"As to Bateman, I have no expectation," Lund Washington to GW, October 1, 1783, "Letters of Lund Washington to George Washington, 1797-1790," typescript, Mount Vernon Ladies' Association of the Union Library, 371.

"everything . . . nessary in the House keeping way," Martha Washington to Fanny Bassett Washington, July 1, 1792, *Worthy Partner,* 239.

PAGE 109

"absolute requirements of my family," GW to Mary Ball Washington, his mother, February 15, 1787, *Writings,* vol. 29: 159.

PAGE 113

"Let the hospitality of the House," GW to Lund Washington, November 26, 1775, *Writings,* vol. 4: 115.

PAGE 115

"Frames for Hot beds [are] to be prepared," GW, "Memorandum of Carpentry Work to be done," June 1791, *Writings,* vol. 31: 308.

"a small roasted pigg, boiled leg of lamb," Frost, "A Day at Mount Vernon," 8.

"digitalis as a cure," William Gordon to GW, January 20, 1787, *Papers,* Confederation Series, vol. 4: 525.

Parsley: A Mount Vernon visitor, Manesseh Cutler, was offered breakfast in January 1802 (before Martha Washington's death). In his diary he mentions dishes "ornamented with sprigs of parsley and other vegetables from the garden." See Mary Thompson, "Herbs/Plants Used or Probably Used at Mount Vernon," manuscript, the Mount Vernon Ladies' Association, n.d.

PAGE 116

the manuscript housekeeping book: See Karen Hess, transcr., *Martha Washington's Booke of Cookery*

(New York: Columbia University Press, 1981, 1995), 447-463; also Thompson, "Herbs/Plants."

PAGE 121

"In the evening G [General] Washington showed us round," Niemcewicz, *Under Their Vine and Fig Tree,* 97.

"12 Bullock Hearts — (a large black May Cherry)," March 21, 1763, *Diaries,* vol. I: 315.

"to give . . . a better appearance as the house [was] approached," GW to Anthony Whiting, April 11, 1792, *Writings,* vol 32: 203.

PAGE 123

"Ladies, the home of Washington is in your charge," Ann Pamela Cunningham, "The Farewell Address of the Founder and First Regent of the Mount Vernon Ladies' Association of the Union," June 1, 1874. The address has been reprinted in every annual report since Cunningham's resignation. The Mount Vernon Ladies' Association Library.

The Mount Vernon Ladies' Association, the first national historic preservation organization and one of the first national women's volunteer organizations, was founded in 1853. Mount Vernon, with 200 acres, was purchased for $200,000 in 1858. For many years the sale of bouquets of "old-time" flowers grown in the gardens provided a major source of revenue.

PAGE 129

"an Abundance of Everything," GW to William Pearce, May 15, 1796, *Writings,* vol. 35: 47.

Chapter Six

PAGE 131

"I am once more seated," GW to Dr. James Anderson, April 7, 1797, *Writings*, vol. 35: 32.

PAGE 132

"Sowed the following Nuts and Seeds," June 13, 1785, *Diaries*, vol. IV: 151.

PAGE 133

"the beautiful prospects which on every side," "Voyage to Barbados," 1751-2, *Diaries*, vol. I: 73.

"Tell the Gardener he must plant," GW to William Pearce, February 22, 1794, *Writings*, vol. 33: 275.

"Does the last, and present years planting," GW to Anthony Whiting, May 5, 1793, *Writings*, vol. 32: 445.

"Under cover of the letter you will receive," GW to Anthony Whiting, February 3, 1793, *Writings*, vol. 32: 318.

PAGE 134

"With respect to field culture of vegetables for cattle," Thomas Jefferson to Tristan Dalton, May 2, 1817, *The Garden and Farm Books of Thomas Jefferson*, ed. Robert C. Baron (Golden, Colo.: Fulcrum, Inc., 1987) 204.

Compleat Body of Husbandry: Thomas Hale, *A Compleat Body of Husbandry* (London: T. Osborne, 1758-59).

PAGE 135

"the controversial political literature of North America," Brookhiser, *Founding Father,* 139.

His agricultural experimentation, as James Flexner writes: Flexner, *Washington,* 47.

"Thermometer at 52 in the Morning," December 7, 1785, *Diaries,* vol. IV: 245. See the introduction to the Diaries, vol. I: XXXIX, for a discussion of Washington's temperature measurements.

"at the very dawn of modern science," Flexner, *Washington,* 47.

"Took the covering off the Plants," April 6, 1786, *Diaries,* vol. IV: 304.

PAGE 136

"The intention of the little garden by the Salt house," GW to Anthony Whiting, February 3, 1793, *Writings,* vol. 32: 328.

PAGE 141

"Gooseberries, the Long iron Coloured," Tobias Lear to GW, February 4, 1794, *Papers,* vol. 265 (January 21–March 15, 1794).

The fruit bushes and trees shipped on board the *Peggy* were expected for months. Washington worried. "I fear the White thorn plants . . . together with Mr. Lears fruit trees, will suffer very much, if they are not entirely destroyed by the advanced season," he wrote to William Pearce [the then manager] at Mount Vernon on May 4. On June 4 their arrival is noted: "The fruit trees . . . arrived at the right time for planting and [William Pearce] . . . hopes that "a great many will live." *Papers,* vol. 267 (May 8–July 12, 1794).

Chapter Seven

PAGE 144

"with yellow buttons and gold epaulettes," GW to James McHenry, Secretary of War, November 13, 1798, *Writings,* vol. 37: 51.

"I shall begrudge no reasonable expense," GW to William Pearce, October 6, 1793, *Writings,* vol. 33: 111.

the bulwark of the war years: Bruce A. Ragsdale, "George Washington, the British Tobacco Trade, and Economic Opportunity in Prerevolutionary Virginia," *The Virginia Magazine of History and Biography* 97, no. 2 (April 1989), 133-162.

Thomas Jefferson once described: Flexner, *Washington,* 191.

PAGE 145

257 bushels in 1764: Alan and Donna Jean Fusonie, *George Washington, Pioneer Farmer* (Mount Vernon: Mount Vernon Ladies' Association, 1998), 9.

PAGE 146

"you will allow he is a farmer of no contemptible scale," Edward Thornton to James Bland Burges, October 3, 1792, S. W. Jackman, "A Young Englishman Reports on the New Nation: Edward Thornton to James Bland Burgess, 1791-1793," *William and Mary Quarterly,* Third Series, 18, no. I (January 1961), 116.

"without seeing something which makes me regret," GW to George William Fairfax, November 10, 1785, *Writings,* vol. 28: 313.

PAGE 148

"to liberate a certain species of property," GW to Tobias Lear, May 6, 1793, *Writings,* vol. 33: 358.

PAGE 149

"The Soil of the tract I am speaking [of]," GW to Arthur Young, December 12, 1793, *Writings,* vol. 33: 176.

PAGE 152

"Midas like . . . convert everything he touches into manure," GW to George William Fairfax, June 30, 1785, *Writings,* vol 28: 186.

"My Estate has been, and probably will continue to be," GW to Thomas Law, May 7, 1798, *Writings,* vol. 36: 257.

PAGE 155

Nine plows, on average: Lois Green Carr and Lorena S. Walsh, "Economic Diversification and Labor Organization in the Chesapeake, 1650-1820," *Work and Labor in Early America,* ed. Stephen Innes (Charlottesville: University Press of Virginia, 1988), 178.

Colonel Landon Carter: See Landon Carter, *Diary of Colonel Landon Carter of Sabine Hall, 1752–1778* (Charlottesville: University Press of Virginia, 1965); also Carr and Walsh, "Economic Diversification," 178-83; Harold B. Gill Jr., "Wheat Culture in Colonial Virginia," *Agricultural History* 52 (July 1978), 380-93.

PAGE 156

"the General has much improved the plan," Jean Jacques Pierre Brissot de Warville, *New Travels in the United States of America Performed in 1788* (Dublin: W. Corbet, 1792), vol. 5: 271-2.

PAGE 157

"equal perhaps to any in America," GW to Arthur Young, December 12, 1793, *Writings,* vol. 33: 176.

The design of the rectangular pit: Dennis J. Pogue, "Archeological Investigations at the Mount Vernon Dung Repository: An Interim Report," Files of the Mount Vernon Ladies' Association Archaeology Department, File Report No. 5, February 1994.

PAGE 161

"the rhetoric of spiritualized and regenerated landscape," Douglas D. C. Chambers, *The Planters of the English Landscape Garden* (New Haven: Yale University Press, 1993), 6.

"storehouse and granary of the world," GW to the Marquis de Lafayette, June 19, 1788, *Writings,* vol. 29: 526.

PAGE 162

"I walk on untrodden ground," GW to Catherine Macaulay Graham, January 9, 1790, *Writings,* vol. 30: 496.

we can agree with one of his biographers, James Flexner: Flexner, *Washington,* 57.

Washington's inability to separate theory from practice: Flexner, *Washington,* 385; see also Wills, *Cincinnatus,* 126, for a discussion of how "classical 'playacting,'" the modeling of behavior on antique models, passed from theory to practice in Washington's day.

PAGE 164

"How many Lambs have you had this Spring?," GW to Lund Washington, March 28, 1781, *Writings,* 21: 386.

Abercombie, John. *The Hot-House Gardener on the General Culture of the Pine-Apple, and Methods of Forcing Early Grapes, Peaches, Nectarines, and Other Choice Fruits,* [etc.]. London: John Stockdale, 1789.

Adams, Abigail. *New Letters of Abigail Adams, 1788–1801.* Edited by Stewart Mitchell. Boston: Houghton Mifflin Company, 1947.

Axelrod, Alan, ed. *The Colonial Revival in America.* New York: W. W. Norton for the Henry Francis du Pont Winterthur Museum, 1985.

Bermingham, Ann. *Landscape and Ideology, The English Rustic Tradition, 1740–1860.* Berkeley: University of California Press, 1986.

Blanchard, Claude. The Journal of Claude Blanchard, Commissary of the French Auxiliary Army sent to the United States during the American Revolution, 1780-1783. Translated by William Duane. Edited by Thomas Balch. Albany, N.Y., 1876. Transcript in a research notebook of early descriptions of Mount Vernon, Mount Vernon Ladies' Association of the Union, n.d.

Bordley, J. B. *Essays and Notes on Husbandry and Rural Affairs.* Philadelphia: Budd and Bartram, 1799.

Brissot de Warville, Jean Jacques Pierre. *New Travels in the United States of America Performed in 1788, vol.* 5. Dublin: W. Corbet, 1792.

Brookhiser, Richard. *Founding Father: Rediscovering George Washington.* New York: The Free Press, 1996.

Brownell, Charles E., Calder Loth, William M. S. Rasmussen, and Richard Guy Wilson. *The Making of Virginia Architecture.* Richmond: Virginia Museum of Fine Arts, 1993.

Carr, Lois Green, and Lorena S. Walsh. "Economic Diversification and Labor Organization in the Chesapeake, 1650-1820." In *Work and Labor in Early America.* Edited by Stephen Innes, 144-188. Chapel Hill: University of North Carolina Press for the Institute of Early American History and Culture, 1988.

Carson, Cary, Ronald Hoffman, and Peter J. Albert. *Of Consuming Interest: The Style of Life in the Eighteenth Century.* Charlottesville: University Press of Virginia for the United States Capitol Historical Society, 1994.

Carter, Edward C., II, John C. Van Horne, and Charles E. Brownell, eds. *Latrobe's Views of America, 1795–1820: Selections from the Watercolors and Sketches.* New Haven: Yale University Press, 1985.

Carter, Landon. *Diary of Colonel Landon Carter of Sabine Hall, 1752–1778.* Edited by Jack P. Greene. Charlottesville: University Press of Virginia, 1965.

Chambers, Douglas D. C. *The Planters of the English Landscape Garden.* New Haven: Yale University Press, 1993.

Clark, Harrison. *All Cloudless Glory, The Life of George Washington.* 2 vols. Washington, D.C.: Regnery Publishing, Inc., 1995.

Dalzell, Robert F., Jr. "Constructing Independence: Monticello, Mount Vernon, and the Men Who Built Them." *Eighteenth-Century Studies* 26, 4 (Summer 1993): 543-80.

de Forest, Elizabeth Kellam. *The Gardens & Grounds at Mount Vernon: How George Washington Planned and Planted Them.* Mount Vernon: The Mount Vernon Ladies' Association of the Union, 1982.

Du Ponceau, Peter Stephen. "The Autobiography of Peter Stephen Du Ponceau." *Pennsylvania Magazine of History and Biography* 63 (July 1939): 311-15.

Epstein, Joseph. "George Washington, An Amateur's View." *The Hudson Review* 51, no. 2 (Spring 1998): 21-39.

Evans, Oliver. *The Young Mill-Wright and Miller's Guide* [etc.] Philadelphia: Lea & Blanchard, 1846. Eleventh edition.

Fithian, Philip Vickers. *Journals and Letters of Philip Vickers Fithian, a Plantation Tutor of the Old Dominion, 1773–1774.* Edited by Hunter Dickinson Farish. Williamsburg: Colonial Williamsburg, 1957.

Reprint, Charlottesville: The University Press of Virginia, 1968, 1996.

Flexner, James Thomas. *Washington: The Indispensable Man.* Boston: Little, Brown and Company, 1969. Reprint, Boston: First Back Bay Edition, 1974.

Frost, Amariah. "A Day At Mount Vernon, in 1797." Edited by Hamilton B. Staples. Worcester, Mass.: 1879. Transcript in a research notebook of early descriptions of Mount Vernon, Mount Vernon Ladies' Association of the Union, n.d.

Fusonie, Alan and Donna Jean. *George Washington, Pioneer Farmer.* Mount Vernon: Mount Vernon Ladies' Association of the Union, 1998.

Hale, Thomas. *A Compleat Body of Husbandry.* London: T. Osborne, 1758-59.

Hess, Karen, transcr. *Martha Washington's Booke of Cookery.* New York: Columbia University Press, 1981. Reprint, 1995.

Hirschfeld, Fritz. *George Washington and Slavery: A Documentary Portrayal.* Columbia: University of Missouri Press, 1997.

Hitt, Thomas. *A Treatise of Fruit-Trees.* London: Printed for the author, 1757.

Hunt, John Dixon, and Peter Willis, eds. *The Genius of the Place: The English Landscape Garden 1620–1820.* New York: Harper & Row, 1975.

Jackman, S. W. "A Young Englishman Reports on

the New Nation: Edward Thornton to James Bland Burgess, 1791-1793." *William and Mary Quarterly,* Third Series, 18, no. 1 (January 1961): 85-121.

Jefferson, Thomas. *The Garden and Farm Books of Thomas Jefferson.* Edited by Robert C. Baron. Golden, Colo.: Fulcrum, Inc., 1987.

Langley, Batty. *New Principles of Gardening: The Laying out and Planting of Parterres, Groves, Wildernesses, Labyrinths, Avenues, Parks, etc. after a more Grand and Rural Manner than has been done before.* London: Printed for A. Bettesworth and J. Batley, 1728.

Latrobe, Benjamin Henry. *The Virginia Journals of Benjamin Henry Latrobe, 1795–1798.* Edited by Edward C. Carter II. New Haven: Yale University Press, 1977.

Leighton, Ann. *American Gardens in the Eighteenth Century: "For Use or For Delight."* Boston: Houghton Mifflin Company, 1976. Reprint, Boston: The University of Massachusetts Press, 1988.

_____. "The Gardens, Grounds and Plants of Mt. Vernon." The Mount Vernon Ladies' Association of the Union, n.d.

Liger d'Auxerre, Louis. *The Compleat Florist, or, The Universal Culture of Flowers, Trees and Shrubs Proper to Embellish Gardens,* [etc.]. With *Le Jardinier Solitaire: The Solitary or Carthusian Gardener, being Dialogues between a Gentleman and a Gard'ner,* by Francis Gentil. London: Benjamin Tooke, 1706.

Maccubbin, Robert P., and Peter Martin, eds. *British and American Gardens in the Eighteenth Century.* Williamsburg: Colonial Williamsburg Foundation, 1984.

Maclay, William. *The Diary of William Maclay and Other Notes on Senate Debates,* vol. 9. Edited by Kenneth R. Bowling and Helen E. Veit. Baltimore: Johns Hopkins University Press, 1988.

Martin, Peter. *The Pleasure Gardens of Virginia, From Jamestown to Jefferson.* Princeton, N.J.: Princeton University Press, 1991.

Miller, Philip. *The Gardener's Dictionary.* 1 vol., abridged. London: For the author, 1771.

_____. *The Gardeners Kalendar.* London: For the author, 1762.

Mount Vernon Ladies' Association of the Union. Annual Reports, 1934, 35, 36, 37. Mount Vernon: Mount Vernon Ladies' Association of the Union.

Nevins, Deborah. "The Gardens." *Antiques Magazine* 135 (February 1989): 524-31.

Niemcewicz, Julian Ursyn. *Under Their Vine and Fig Tree: Travels through America in 1797–1799, 1805 with some further account of life in New Jersey,* vol. 14. Edited and translated by Metchie J. E. Budka. Elizabeth, N.J.: Grassman Publishing Co., 1965.

Norton, J. Dean, and Susanne A. Schrage-Norton. "The Upper Garden at Mount Vernon Estate, Its Past, Present, and Future: A Reflection of Eighteenth-Century Gardening; Phase II, The Complete Report." Mount Vernon Ladies' Association of the Union, 1985.

Owen, Scott Campbell. "George Washington's Mount Vernon as Anglo-Palladian Architecture" (master's thesis, University of Virginia, 1991).

Peters, Richard. "Remarks on the Plan of a Stercorary," in *Memoirs of the Philadelphia Society for Promoting Agriculture.* 281–85. Philadelphia: Jane Aitkin, 1808.

Pogue, Dennis J. "Archeological Investigations at the Mount Vernon Dung Repository: An Interim Report." The Mount Vernon Ladies' Association of the Union, 1994.

_____. "Giant in the Earth: George Washington, Landscape Designer." In *Landscape Archeology: Reading and Interpreting the American Historical Landscape,* edited by R. Yamin and K. Bescherer Metheny. 52–69. Knoxville: University of Tennessee Press, 1996.

Ragsdale, Bruce A. "George Washington, the British Tobacco Trade, and Economic Opportunity in Prerevolutionary Virginia," *The Virginia Magazine of History and Biography* 97, no. 2 (April 1989): 133–162.

Sayen, Guthrie. "George Washington's 'Unmannerly' Behavior." Paper presented at the George Washington Symposium, Mount Vernon, 1997.

Schrage-Norton, Suzanne A. "Nursery and Fruit Garden Research Report." Mount Vernon Ladies' Association of the Union, n.d.

A Society of Gentlemen, Members of the Society for the Encouragement of Arts, Manufactures, and Commerce. *The Complete Farmer: or, a General Dictionary of Husbandry in All its Branches;* [etc.]. London: Printed for the authors, 1769, 1793 editions.

Sobel, Mechal. *The World They Made Together. Black and White Values in Eighteenth-Century Virginia.* Princeton, N.J.: Princeton University Press, 1987.

Thompson, Mary. "Herbs/Plants Used or Probably Used at Mount Vernon." The Mount Vernon Ladies' Association of the Union, n.d.

Wall, Charles C., Christine Meadows, John H. Rhodehamel, and Ellen McCallister Clark. *Mount Vernon, A Handbook.* Mount Vernon: The Mount Vernon Ladies' Association of the Union, 1974. Fifth printing, 1995.

Washington, George. "A List of Ornamental Trees and Shrubs Noted in the Writings of George Washington." Compiled and edited by Robert B. Fisher. The Mount Vernon Ladies' Association of the Union, 1945–79.

_____. *The Diaries of George Washington.* Edited by Donald Jackson and Dorothy Twohig. 6 vols. Charlottesville: University Press of Virginia, 1976–79.

_____. *The Writings of George Washington.* Edited by John C. Fitzpatrick. 39 vols. Washington, D.C.: United States Government Printing Office, 1931–40.

Washington, Martha. "*Worthy Partner," The Papers of Martha Washington.* Compiled by Joseph E. Fields. Westport, Conn.: Greenwood Press, 1994.

Weld, Isaac. *Travels through the States of North America and the Provinces of Upper and Lower Canada, during the years 1795, 1796, and 1797,* vol. 1. London: John Stockdale, 1799.

Williams, Morley Jeffers. "Washington's Changes at Mount Vernon Plantation." *Landscape Architecture* 28, no. 2 (January 1938): 61–73.

Wills, Garry. *Cincinnatus: George Washington and the Enlightenment.* Garden City, N.Y.: Doubleday and Co., 1984.

Wood, Gordon S. "The Greatness of George Washington." *The Virginia Quarterly Review* 68 (Spring 1992): 189–207.

Zakim, Michael. "What Is a Political History of Clothing?" *Columbia Library Columns* 46, no. 1 (Spring 1997): 33–37.

Poplar, 73
    tulip, *55, 68, 70*
Poppy, *99*
    oriental, *91*
Potato, 137, 155
Potomac River
    Great Falls of, *58*
    and landscape design, 37
    photographs of, *12, 19, 26–27,*
        54–55, 165
    as property line, *38, 39*
The Practical Farmer (John Spurrier), 157
Pride-of-Barbados, 133
Pride of China, 132, *138–9*
Primula × polyantha, 91
Prince Nurseries, 67
Privet, 132, 135
Pumpkin, 137
Purple chard, *126–7*
Purple coneflower, *92*

Quince, 121

Radish, 91, *102*
Rappahannock River, 38, 39
Raspberry, *107,* 115, 121
Redbud
    in landscape planting, 13, 29, 63, 73
    photographs of, *12, 13, 52, 55, 62, 100–101*
Regnier, Claude *(The Farmer),* 163
Revolutionary War, 36, 38-40. *See also*

American Revolution
Ribes sativum, 120
Richardt, Joachim Ferdinand *(Mount Vernon),*
    128
Rivers
    Charles, 64
    Hudson, 58, 59
    Potomac *(See* Potomac River)
    Rappahannock, *38, 39*
Robertson, Walter *(George Washington),* 162
Robinia pseudoacacia, 20, 50, 68
Rocket double larkspur, *90*
Roman nectarine, *103*
Roosevelt, Franklin D., 10
Roque's Burnett grass, *22*
Rosa
    eglanteria, 71
    gallica versicolor, 92
    'Celsiana', *91*
    mundi, *92*
Rose, 29, 91, 94, 115
    European guelder, 70
Rose campion, *91, 93*
Rosemary, *15,* 91
Rose-of-Sharon, 70
Royal Gift (Spanish jackass), 19
Rudbeckia
    hirta, 28, 96
Rye, 155
Sabal umbraculifera, 66
Sage, 118

Salix
    alba 'Vitellina', 70
    babylonica, 68, 70
Santolina, 108, *126–7*
Santolina
    chamaecyparissus, 108
    rosmarinifolia, 108
Sargent, Charles Sprague, 68
Sargent, Winthrop, 91
Sassafras, 63, 73
Savage, Edward, 45, 57
Savoy cabbage, 91
Scottish furze, 137
Seed collection, 96
Setting stick, *132*
Shaddock, *94, 95*
Shaftesbury, Lord, 36
Southern catalpa, 67
Southern magnolia, 68, 70, *100–101, 138–9*
Spades, *105*
The Spectator (Joseph Addison), 55, 173
Spinach, 115
Spotswood, Alexander, 143
Spurrier, John, 157
Squash, crookneck, *129*
Stachys byzantina, 99
Stamp Act (1765), 145
Stearns, Junius Brutus *(The Farmer),* 163
Stercorary, 157
Stone fruit, 103, *120,* 121
Straw bell, *136*